The Wesley Challenge

The Wesley Challenge:
21 Days to a More Authentic Faith

The Wesley Challenge

978-1-5018-3290-1
978-1-5018-3291-8 eBook

The Wesley Challenge: DVD

978-1-5018-3294-9

The Wesley Challenge: Leader Guide

978-1-5018-3292-5
978-1-5018-3293-2 eBook

The Wesley Challenge: Youth Study Book

978-1-5018-3298-7
978-1-5018-3299-4 eBook

The Wesley Challenge: Campaign Download Package

978-1-5018-3300-7

CHRIS FOLMSBEE

the WESLEY challenge

21 DAYS TO A MORE AUTHENTIC FAITH

Abingdon Press / Nashville

The Wesley Challenge
21 Days to a More Authentic Faith

This book is printed on elemental chlorine-free paper.

ISBN 978-1-5018-3290-1

Scripture quotations are taken from the Common English Bible, copyright 2011. Used by permission. All rights reserved..

17 18 19 20 21 22 23 24 25 26 — 10 9 8 7 6 5 4 3 2 1

MANUFACTURED IN THE UNITED STATES OF AMERICA

Dedicated to the amazing people of The United Methodist Church of the Resurrection. I am grateful for the opportunity to serve you as we all strive to become deeply committed Christians. Enjoy the journey of knowing, loving, and serving God!

CONTENTS

FOREWORD

If you visit Lincoln College at Oxford University, and you ask around, you'll be shown a second-floor room, overlooking the green. Step inside and you'll find a room intended to capture the birthplace of Methodism. Here John Wesley, an instructor or fellow of Lincoln College, would meet with a handful of undergraduate students, including Charles, his younger brother, to study Scripture, to pray, to read and reflect upon other works on the Christian life, and to encourage one another in their pursuit of the Christian life. John would later call these meetings, "the first rise of Methodism."

The meetings were not an end in themselves. They were intended to so shape the soul of participants that their everyday lives were changed. And changed they were. This small band of Christians sought to, in the words of Wesley, have "the love of God shed abroad in his heart by the Holy Ghost given unto him." They sought to love God and love their neighbor. Their faith moved beyond the walls of the university, and it was seen in their service to the poor, visiting the prisoners, and love for their fellow human beings.

It's been said that among the most important things leaders do is ask the right questions. Wesley had learned from others the value of asking questions of one's spiritual life. Among the best-known advocates for the practice of critical self-examination through probing questions was the sixteenth-century priest, Saint Ignatius of Loyola. His "daily examen" continues to guide the spiritual life of millions of believers. Wesley and the early Methodists developed several sets of questions aimed at helping Christians grow deeper and to become "all together Christian."

Among the practices of those earliest Methodists was the asking of one another a series of twenty-one (or twenty-two) questions intended to strip away pretense, expose the motives of the heart, and lead toward a holiness. The truth be told, I had read these questions on several occasions, but I had not spent much time thinking about them. But one day, Chris Folmsbee, with whom I have the privilege of serving at The United Methodist Church of the Resurrection, came to my office excited about an idea. He said that he believed the questions asked among the Oxford Methodists might have value for Christians today.

Chris was not the first to suggest this, but he was the first person I knew to be so passionate that he began to map out a plan to help our church, and other churches, reclaim these powerful questions. He asked if I would consider setting aside three weeks in our church's calendar to preach on these twenty-one questions. He had already grouped Wesley's questions into three broad categories which would form the basis of the three weeks of sermons. He and his team prepared twenty-one daily readings to go along with each of the questions.

Our congregation was energized by this three-week emphasis. We had thousands who were reading and reflecting upon the daily question and devotional that was prepared to go with it. Our small groups and classes met together to ask each other the questions and to ponder their meaning. The small group I am in used the material and found it to be challenging and refreshing.

At the end of the three weeks, I felt we'd moved our congregation forward in the Christian life. We were more cognizant of our own shortcomings, had a deeper desire to become the people God wanted us to be, and had invited the Holy Spirit's help in forming us into authentic Christ-followers.

The truth is that the pursuit of these questions through the study you hold in your hand is not something that is "once and done." Wesley and the Oxford Methodists continued asking these questions over and over and over again. My hunch, and hope, is that you will return to this book again and again as you seek to become the Christian God intends for you to be.

Adam Hamilton

INTRODUCTION

I've spent the better part of my adult life looking for consistent ways to develop my spiritual life and continuing my journey of becoming a deeply committed Christian. I've tried and tried to develop disciplines or habits that help me live into God's intention for my life—to live a whole life, a life of total love for God and others. This pursuit has led me to be steadfastly aware of my relationship with God, my relationship with myself, and, of course, my relationship with others.

I am sure you have also figured out in your spiritual journey that in order for something to become a pattern or habit, you have to work to simply *do it*. Whatever it is—prayer, fasting, simplicity, solitude—you have to consciously and consistently act over and over again for a desired virtue to become a way of life.

This is not just true in the spiritual life. For example, a baseball player must repeatedly hit balls off a tee or in a batting cage for hours and hours to develop the muscle memory that leads to hitting in a game. A pilot must fly a certain number of hours so that the necessary reading of the instruments and the proper turning of the dials and flipping of the switches become second nature in order for the pilot to make quick, correct decisions. Would you want to fly with a pilot who doesn't have the mandatory flight time recorded? Preachers or public speakers must practice the fundamentals of effective communication skills many times before they would be considered "one with" the art of speaking or preaching.

This is true of all people in all stages of life. My son, for example, who is currently thirteen, is an expert at video games. He didn't get to be an expert by playing one game, one time, if you know what I mean. To master a craft or skill we must do three things—practice, practice, and practice—and we must be disciplined to do it regularly.

To develop a guiding set of personal life virtues (or Christian practices), experimenting with ideas and exercises is necessary. We don't value something because we say we do. We value something because what we do shows that we value it. I do not merely love my wife and children because I say I love them. Rather, my actions show that my devotion to them is more than merely empty words. I have a hearing-impaired son. When he was young, around three to four years old, I could not simply say "I love you" to him. I had to demonstrate my love for him with a smile, a kiss, a hug, a high five, a kind gesture—something that went beyond words. Similarly, to move forward in our spiritual journey of a life of total love for God and others, we must act repeatedly.

This short book is about going beyond words to develop the spiritual habits, practices, and actions that can lead toward a thriving Christian life. It is about committing the next twenty-one days to experimenting with and testing the twenty-one questions John and Charles Wesley used with the group that was nicknamed "The Holy Club." If you look at the historical record, you might find twenty-one, twenty-two, or even as many as twenty-four questions that people trace back nearly three hundred years and attribute to John Wesley.

I've chosen to construct a set of twenty-one of those questions—three weeks' worth. I hope that this book, and the supplemental resources, help you find what I have found through the twenty-one questions—a sustainable union with God through everyday practices that grow out of the daily actions we choose. I've learned through my life of pursuing a total love for God and others that the gospel of Jesus Christ is both proclaimed and performed. To become the new creatures God desires that we become, we must both talk about and live out the teachings of Jesus.

What exactly is the Holy Club?

The Holy Club, as it was derisively termed by unconvinced fellow students and faculty in Oxford, was a group of people who devoted their time to Bible study, serving the poor, giving to those in need, visiting prisoners, reading the classics and considering them together, fasting, and, of course, prayer.

In 1729, the Holy Club was officially formed in Christ Church, Oxford, England. Charles Wesley formed the group to practice spiritual methods that would provide the group with a rhythm or contour for their faith development. Charles wanted to make certain that his values were not merely developed due to his upbringing and his own personal study. He wanted to be sure that he and others arrived at their beliefs and convictions by working them out in everyday life. He recruited his brother John Wesley to lead the group, because of his wisdom, experience, and leadership. John led the group until 1735.

This 21-day challenge is not about joining a holy club

This book isn't about joining a "holy club," as Wesley's contemporaries dubbed it. Rather, it is about opening our minds, our hearts, and our hands to develop a lifestyle of practicing the disciplines of our Christian faith. We choose to commit to these practices in order that we might, through our deepening spiritual union with God, bear witness to God's work in the world. The point of these practices is not to make you appear holy. Instead, committing to the practices that emerge from Wesley's questions is an effort to help our family and friends, and all those we come into contact with, find and follow Jesus.

How to use this book for your spiritual growth

Over the next twenty-one days we'll work with each of one of Wesley's twenty-one questions. Each day you'll contemplate a different question. You'll also be given some reflection on one person's interpretation of meanings behind the questions. Each day you'll receive a number of discussion questions and a few practical ideas that will help you (and those in your group) develop a healthy, sustainable rhythm of faithful Christian living. (It is likely you won't have time, especially when you discuss this with others, to cover every question asked. That is totally OK. It is more important to have meaningful conversation than to race through answering as many questions as you possibly can.) The goal is to make the Christian practices into a routine, forming a way of life that reveals a total love for God and others.

Research shows that it takes twenty-one days to develop a habit. I pray that you'll be disciplined to stick to the readings and practices over the next twenty-one days, forming a deeper relationship with God, self, and others and ultimately increasing the frequency and duration of the devout moments in your life.

The importance of engaging this book with others

Finally, I hope you'll choose to participate in this 21-day challenge in the context of a group. Discipleship happens best in community. This book certainly can be engaged in individually. However, the Wesleys originally intended the practices that resulted from the soul-searching to be lived out in a band of brothers and sisters. Our faith is lived out, not in isolation, but with others. Jesus modeled this for us when he selected a small group of young people to invest in. This group of disciples, therefore, grew in their knowledge of Jesus together, in community.

Section 1

RELATIONSHIP WITH GOD: AN UPWARD FOCUS

Section 1

RELATIONSHIP WITH GOD: AN UPWARD FOCUS

Authentic followers of Jesus are not content simply to learn ideas about God. Rather, authentic followers of Jesus observe, study, internalize, and eventually adopt the teachings and actions, or the virtues, of Jesus. In the end, therefore, the theology of faithful Christians is progressively applied into every dimension of the Christian's life, making it known not only by mere words but also by actions of vulnerable love.

Christian practices shape us, and Wesley knew that for one to be truly shaped into the image of God it would require a commitment to practices or methods such as prayer and Bible reading and study.

It is important to note that living out Christian practices is not what leads us to holiness. Praying and reading a Bible in order to check off a list or fulfill a supposed duty is not what Wesley (or Jesus, for that matter) had in mind. Instead, through a lasting commitment to practices, we are gradually formed into the true image in which we've been purposely created.

When Christians learn to practice Christianity in the way of Jesus, it turns them upward. This means that our focus becomes our relationship with God. Maturing Christians seek to please God with their whole life. Christians do not practice Christianity for the sake of helping themselves first, but instead to align themselves with God's mission in the world. We have been created that we might faithfully live into our purpose—to reflect God's radiant and extravagant love.

Over the next few days you will be challenged to read, think, reflect, pray, and live out actions that reveal what it means to turn your focus upward, toward God. Through the various readings and practices, you will be challenged to develop a lifestyle marked first by your intentions to turn your heart upward and second by your ongoing actions that demonstrate that your relationship with God is growing and vibrant. This growing and vibrant life of faith is not to reveal your own pious life, but rather a God who is love.

In the seven questions you will interact with over the following days, Wesley set forth a challenge to become who God created us to be. We most clearly see who we were created to be in the person and work of Jesus. As you prepare to embark on the coming challenges, know that in the person and work of Jesus, you have been given the blueprint necessary for the life God intended for you to live.

Chapter 1

IS JESUS REAL TO ME?

A few months ago I spent ten days trekking through the fifth gospel—The Holy Land, Israel. People refer to the Holy Land as the fifth gospel because when you are there, in the midst of all of the history, geography, tradition, and religion, the four Gospels of Matthew, Mark, Luke, and John come alive in new ways, ways that just reading the text cannot bring you. Jesus was made more real to me in Israel, and as a result, Jesus is more real to me today than ever before in my life.

I believe Wesley's question, "Is Jesus real to me?" may be the most important of all. As we reflect on this question, we see that it gets at the point of our Christian pursuit of holiness and witness. Jesus is real to us when Jesus is tangible to others through our words, actions, disciplines, and practices. Jesus is made real to us, and to others around us, when our trust relationship with Jesus is incomparably more important than just knowing facts and rules in a religion *about* Jesus.

Acts chapter 8 tells the beautiful story of an Ethiopian eunuch who is returning from the Temple, from worshiping God. The eunuch is reading one of the scrolls of Isaiah. The Holy Spirit moves and directs Philip to the eunuch on a road in the Judean wilderness to help the eunuch understand what he is reading. When asked, "Do you understand what you are reading?" the eunuch's response is, "How can I unless someone explains it to me?" Philip was sent to help the eunuch make sense of what he was reading. Acts 8:35 tells us that Philip explains to the eunuch that the passage of Isaiah he is reading relates to the good news about Jesus.

The Ethiopian had pilgrimaged to Jerusalem to experience a religion that was outside of his personal heritage. As a eunuch, he wasn't even supposed to be present in the Temple. His new understanding, thanks to Philip's attention to the promptings of the Holy Spirit, did not limit his participation to believing the Jewish laws or a distant God. Instead, Philip helps the eunuch understand that Jesus is a person, not a proposition. Jesus was made real through the story of God in Isaiah, Philip's obedient witness, and through the eunuch's newfound belief in an accessible, real Jesus.

In asking this question, Wesley wants Christians to make sure that we are not simply partaking in a religion, but that we are experiencing a relationship with Jesus. For Jesus to be real to us there must be more than a mere nod of the head, so to speak. There must also be a trail of tangible evidence that we leave everywhere we go that helps people find what we have—a genuine, sustainable relationship with Jesus, the Christ.

On the western side of the Sea of Galilee, a few miles north of Tiberias, there is a mountain called Mount Arbel. From Mount Arbel, you can see the entire Sea of Galilee region. It was there that Jesus and the Gospel stories became real to me in a way I had never experienced before. From Mount Arbel you can visualize how Jesus' ministry would have been carried out, on foot and by boat. You see Capernaum to the northeast and envision how possible it would have been for the stories of Jesus to be real. From a child hearing the stories of Jesus in Sunday school to an adult hearing the stories of Jesus taught in seminary, I had always believed in Jesus, but not to the depth I now believe. The fifth gospel experience I have had by visiting Israel has changed the way I view many of the stories of Jesus' teaching, miracles, and prayers. When the lens through which we see the world changes, Jesus is made more real.

Jesus becomes more real to us each day when we participate in the process of becoming more deeply committed Christians through the practices of discipleship. Scripture reading, study, prayer, mission work, fasting, moments of solitude, submission to the mission of God's will for our life, and joining authentic community all change the lens through which we view the world. As we view the world in new ways, we can continue in our pursuit of holiness and witness by allowing Jesus to be made real to us. *Is Jesus real to you?*

Today's Challenge

Make Jesus real for someone you come in contact with today. Notice the needs of people around you with a heightened awareness, and then bravely act as Christ would act.

Discipleship, and the path the church uses to help people become deeply committed Christians, isn't about outward piety. Rather, discipleship in the way of Jesus is about experiencing a person. By trusting in Jesus, and as a result of that relationship, living out all that Jesus modeled for us is the goal of the Christian life. If the goal of the Christian life is to be as Christ is, then Christ must be real to us.

Reflection Questions

1. When has Jesus seemed the most real to you in your life? The least real? What were those circumstances?
2. How can you make Jesus seem more real to you *now*? What discipleship practices can you put into place in your life to become a more deeply committed Christian?
3. Who has been the Philip in your life, helping you to understand the good news about Jesus? Are you fulfilling that role in someone else's life?

Personal Application Ideas

1. Review the ways in which you are experiencing spiritual growth. Is it time to add additional dimensions to your journey to help deepen your faith and make Christ more

real to you? Choose one practice that you don't typically engage in, such as fasting, or serving in the inner city. Investigate your options and incorporate this practice more regularly into your spiritual life.

2. Make a pilgrimage to a holy place or a place of Christian significance. If the Holy Land isn't a feasible option for you, brainstorm a destination that might be. Perhaps it's a beautiful local cathedral, where the stained glass tells Christ's story in a breathtaking way. Or perhaps the birthplace of people who dedicated themselves to living as Christ lived would be interesting. Use your imagination!

---

scripture

God so loved the world that he gave his only Son, so that everyone who believes in him won't perish but will have eternal life.

John 3:16

Prayer

Everlasting God,
Who is your beloved Son,
Who is the King of the whole world;
Who wills to restore all things to be made new;
Who gives mercy to all the people of all the nations,
Who with you, God, lives and reigns for ever,
we ask that we find Jesus to be more real every day.
Amen.

Chapter 2

AM I ENJOYING PRAYER?

When I was a kid, I learned to pray using the acronym ACTS: Adoration, Confession, Thanksgiving, and Supplication. I've used this model of prayer most of my adult life in both my individual prayer times and the times of corporate prayer I've led. I find the outline of prayer to be something I can focus on, move through, and celebrate.

To be honest, I am not exactly sure what Wesley meant with this question. What's more, I've never really wondered if I am enjoying prayer. The more I ponder Wesley's question, however, the more I find profound worth in it. To enjoy prayer is to simply have a good experience of prayer. Be it daily, hourly, or occasionally, prayer is meant to be a positive and enriching worship experience. I use the word *experience* to highlight the fact that an experience is different from a task or a duty. An experience involves insight gained from a practice. To pray and enjoy it, therefore, is to regularly engage in the practice of prayer and as a result develop a deeper understanding of God, self, others, and the world.

I love John 17, the chapter that many people call Jesus' High Priestly Prayer. Some scholars and theologians also refer to this prayer as simply, "The Prayer of Jesus" or "The Real Lord's Prayer." Within this prayer, I think we can gain insight and develop perspective about what Wesley meant when he challenged his fellow group members with the question, "Am I enjoying prayer?"

Remember, I am proposing that to "enjoy" prayer is not necessarily to find prayer pleasing or to delight in it, although you may. I am proposing that to enjoy prayer, according to Wesley, is to have experiences of discovery within the practice. We may often find prayer pleasing and a delight. However, some prayer is painful. Have you ever cried out to God in anger? That is a prayer experience. Have you ever questioned God with a loud cry of "Why?" That is also prayer. The moments that led you to that prayer were not likely pleasing and delightful, but I believe you may still "enjoy" prayer.

In the High Priestly Prayer in John 17, we find that Jesus' prayer was meant to do four things. First, Jesus' prayer was meant to bring glory to God. I believe that Jesus found enjoyment in worshiping God. Second, Jesus prays for himself and that through his actions he might bring glory to God. Again, Jesus enjoyed his prayer that he might bring God glory. Third, Jesus prays for his friends, the disciples. With the love Jesus consistently demonstrated to his disciples, I have to imagine that Jesus also found fulfillment in this part of the prayer. Finally, Jesus prays for those yet to come, those who will be impacted by the ministry of the disciples as the Holy Spirit leads them. This prayer was a prayer of enjoyment.

Are you familiar with what happens next in the Gospel of John? Jesus is betrayed and arrested, not exactly a joyful time for Jesus and the disciples. To "enjoy" prayer is to experience God through realizing and remembering God, self, others, and the world, and at the same time trust the direction God desires for our lives.

When we think of prayer and ponder the question, "Am I enjoying prayer?" I believe there are at least five key practices that can lead us toward enjoying prayer. These practices are not hard and fast rules; they are suggested methods we can use to help us better establish a consistent and faithful approach to regular prayer.

1. **Find a routine and a regular place to pray.** I find it helpful in my prayer times to have a routine or a framework. Have you ever started to pray and then been

distracted by the one hundred things you have going on? Me too. The ACTS framework that I mentioned at the beginning of this chapter has helped me to remain present and focused. I have also found a great deal of help in praying in the same place each day—my family room while I am drinking my morning coffee. What's the best place for you to pray?

Today's Challenge

Memorize this one sentence prayer: "Lord Jesus Christ, son of the living God, have mercy on me, a sinner." Repeat the sentence throughout the day, saying it more than once each time you pray it.

2. **Schedule time(s) in the day to pray.** I use the ACTS framework in the morning when I pray. However, I also use a mobile phone app that allows me to liturgically read prayers three times a day—morning, midday, and evening. Sometimes I read a sentence or two and sometimes I read all of the prayers for that day and time. I have found that setting my alarm on my phone gives me breaks in the day in which to remind myself of God's faithfulness and to enjoy prayer.

3. **Pray with others and for others.** I have a very small— only three of us—men's group that I pray with. It helps me to have others to pray with and for. This way I am held accountable, and at the same time I can humbly participate in the lives of others.

4. **Memorize one-sentence prayers.** "Not mine, but yours, Oh, Lord" and "Lord Jesus Christ, son of the living God, have mercy on me, a sinner" are two of the sentence prayers that I have memorized and say on occasion. Sometimes I will even find myself praying them in the rhythm of my breathing, while doing the most mundane tasks like e-mail correspondence. Sentence prayers help us to "pray without ceasing," as the Apostle Paul taught, meaning our heart or our spirit is always in a manner of enjoying prayer.

5. **Cultivate an attitude of humility.** When you pray, pray knowing that God is God and we are not. When we pray, we pray meekly, knowing that God is King and we are God's servants. Ask boldly and confidently because you do, after all, serve a powerful God. However, in your boldness and your confidence seek a posture of listening and learning, not telling and doing.

To enjoy prayer is to experience God and in doing so discover a deeper sense of union with God. We pray to lean into God's goodness and strength. When we pray well, we learn to enjoy it.

Reflection Questions

1. Were you taught how to pray as a child? If so, who taught you, and what were you instructed to do?
2. What kind of routine or schedule do you currently follow in your prayer life?
3. Think about a time when you prayed in earnest. What were the circumstances surrounding that time of prayer? What did you feel when the prayer was completed?

Personal Application Ideas

1. Commit to establishing a prayer routine. Pick a quiet place in your home or office. Pray at the same time each day. Start simply, dedicating just a few minutes at first. Use the ACTS model or any method that leads you toward the experience of enjoying prayer.
2. Download a prayer app or sign up for a daily devotional e-mail. Use the prayers and devotions from these tools in your scheduled prayer time, or use them as ways to supplement your prayer experiences throughout the day.
3. Pray in a way that works for you. If you enjoy writing, you may want to keep a prayer journal and write out your prayers. You may want to pray out loud. You might want to pray as you walk or exercise. Find the ways that lead you to richer experiences.

scripture

Jesus told them, "When you pray, say:

> 'Father, uphold the holiness of your name.
> Bring in your kingdom.
> Give us the bread we need for today.
> Forgive us our sins,
>   for we also forgive everyone who has wronged us.
> And don't lead us into temptation.'"

Luke 11:2-4

Prayer

Answer me when I cry out, my righteous God!
*   Set me free from my troubles!*
*   Have mercy on me!*
*   Listen to my prayer!*

Psalm 4:1

Each of us has been created for good, and when we don't reflect this image of goodness and choose to practice harmful, sinful habits, we don't live into the story God has designed for us.

Chapter 3

DO I INSIST UPON DOING SOMETHING ABOUT WHICH MY CONSCIENCE IS UNEASY?

When I was a kid I developed a very bad, harmful habit. I was a shoplifter. I used to steal the things I wanted that I couldn't pay for. At one point it got to be such a bad habit that nearly every time I walked into a department store I would walk out with a toy, a game, a music CD, whatever I wanted. Every time I mustered up the courage to practice my sinful craft of shoplifting, I would get a funny feeling in the pit of my stomach.

Even though this knot in my stomach was real, I insisted upon forging past my uneasy conscience and continuing my harmful, sinful habit. I did this for several years (into my early teenage years) until one day I was caught. My parents were called into the store, the police were called to the scene, and my seemingly nice-kid front was destroyed as people found out I was a thief. Even today as I write this I am incredibly embarrassed and humiliated by my actions of more than thirty years ago. I know I am forgiven and that God's grace has given me freedom from those instances of wrongdoing. However, I still get knots in my stomach when I speak of it. Those "knots in my stomach," I believe, are my conscience reminding me that what I did was wrong.

Last week I had a conversation with someone I know who admitted a long-term addiction to pornography. As we talked about his damaging habit he said, "I know it is wrong because every time I turn my browser toward the websites I shouldn't be looking at, I get an uneasy feeling of wrongdoing. My conscience is telling me no and yet I insist on proceeding anyway."

The feelings we get when we insist on doing something we shouldn't—gossiping, lusting, lying, stealing, cheating—signal the goodness in us battling with the human desire to usurp God's authority and be in charge of our own life. Each of us has been created for good, and when we don't reflect this image of goodness and choose to practice harmful, sinful habits, we don't live into the story God has designed for us. This is why we have uneasy consciences. We are meant for good, not bad, and the Holy Spirit reminds us of his presence in our lives and our design for goodness each time we choose to rebel against God's design for our lives.

Mark Twain once said, "An uneasy conscience is like a hair in the mouth." Meaning, when we are not doing what we *should* be doing, and when we are doing what we *shouldn't*, an uneasy conscience provides us with that annoying, unpleasant feeling that something isn't right. When something isn't right, we are aware in many ways. The question is, therefore, what are we going to do with the "hair in our mouth"? Are we going to remove it or let it continue annoying us, reminding us of our shortcoming?

It is important to remember that our upbringing and social norms can shape our conscience. For example, a child raised in an organized crime family might find his conscience uneasy if he decided to tell law enforcement about an illegal act he had seen. That's why Bible reading and prayer are so important. Through these practices, God can shape or reshape our conscience to accurately reflect God's good purposes for our life.

The Bible teaches in many places that God wants our very best. God wants us to live into our humanity by living as Jesus lived—holy. Our goal as Christians is to increase the frequency and duration of the holy moments in our lives. Properly trained, the uneasy conscience we feel is a reminder, a whisper if you will, that what we are about to do or leave undone is a direct choice we are making that is in conflict with increasing the frequency and duration of the holy moments in our lives.

So how, then, can we avoid the uneasy conscience and choose to live into the goodness in which we have been created?

> ### Today's Challenge
>
> Tell a trusted friend about a temptation you are struggling with. Name it, and ask for your friend's help in holding you accountable in working to overcome what is causing your "uneasy conscience."

Here are five ways to live into that goodness by overcoming the temptation in our lives:

1. **Realize your areas of weakness and admit them to a friend/group.** All of us have areas in our lives that make it hard to live into the goodness we were designed to live into. For some it is money, sex, or power. For others it is overeating or gossip. What are the areas of your life that you can easily feel yourself leaning toward? Name those areas and admit them to others so that they can help you overcome them.

2. **Recognize where the temptation is coming from.** What is the source of the temptation? Again, is it a desire for money, sex, or power? Is the urge a result of getting burned by another and wanting to take revenge? Is it coming from a place of discontent or cynicism or hate? Once you locate the sources of your temptations, you can more readily combat them.

3. **Imagine the consequences of such a decision.** Have you ever thought to yourself, "If I make this decision, it could mean what?" That's what the uneasy feeling or the Spirit's

presence in your life is demanding from you. Think about it. Do you really want to embarrass yourself? Do you really want to bring harm to another? Do you really want to bring another down? Think about the consequences of your potential actions. Take advantage of the uneasy conscience reminding you that the outcomes are likely not meant for good.

4. **Reorder your life accordingly.** Take the necessary steps in your life that eliminate or minimize the temptation. Tempted to spend money on something you don't need to make yourself feel better? Then leave your credit cards in the kitchen drawer. Can't seem to overcome your desire to "power trip"? Then intentionally place yourself in an environment where you have to serve others.

5. **Meditate on God's Word and pray daily.** I learned a very simple "breath" prayer a few years back. The prayer is simply, "My help comes from the Lord, the maker of heaven and earth." The prayer comes from Psalm 121 and has been prayed by Christians for hundreds of years. This prayer helps me each and every day as it has become ingrained into my head and heart. Other times in my life I have memorized short Scripture passages or parts of long passages, and as I feel tempted to act on a desire, I repeat the passage out loud. This helps remind me that God is God and I am not.

Although annoying at times, the rightly trained uneasy conscience is a good thing. It reminds us that we are called to live into the goodness in which we were created. To insist on doing something that our conscience tells us we shouldn't do is to willfully choose to ignore God's desire for goodness. To insist on working to increase the frequency and duration of the holy moments in our life is to live honoring and glorifying God. Which will it be?

Reflection Questions

1. Do you have areas of your life that are causing you an uneasy conscience? What are these weaknesses?
2. Dig deeply—what is driving these temptations in your life? What steps can you put into place to combat the temptations you are facing?

Personal Application Ideas

1. Every time you find yourself leaning in to a temptation, ask yourself the questions: "What are the consequences of giving in to this weakness? Who may be hurt by this? Will the satisfaction of this moment be worth the consequences I may face?" Force yourself to answer the questions before you act.
2. Identify one area of your life causing you an uneasy conscience. Think through how you can reorder your life to minimize or eliminate this temptation.

---

scripture

From now on, brothers and sisters, if anything is excellent and if anything is admirable, focus your thoughts on these things: all that is true, all that is holy, all that is just, all that is pure, all that is lovely, and all that is worthy of praise.

Philippians 4:8

Prayer

God, you alone know the true condition of my heart. Although I may be able to trick others with my words and actions, I know that you know the truth and are not fooled. Lead me to do and say only what is pleasing in your sight so that I might live according to your purposes. Amen.

The Bible is a love story—
the story of a loving, creative
God who is good. It is a
collection of wonderfully
engaging stories...meant not
just to amuse or entertain,
but to shape the very life we live.

Chapter 4

DID THE BIBLE LIVE IN ME TODAY?

I memorized much of the Bible as a kid. I can still remember receiving prizes in Sunday school—a piece of candy, a star next to my name on the board, or a blindfolded selection from the box of small and inexpensive toys. For most of my early life I valued the Bible highly. Looking back, however, it was valuable mostly because it typically paid off in some form of indulgence.

As I matured into my middle and late teens, the Bible became less valuable to me. Somewhere along the line it became a rule book that I primarily understood as keeping me from exploring and experimenting in life's great fun. Perhaps it was my teenage rebellion that turned me off to the Bible? Perhaps it was the way the adults in my life used the Bible to try to influence or even correct my ways? Actually, it was probably a combination of the two. Regardless of the reasons, I felt distant from the stories I heard as a kid that seemed to put God on par with Santa Claus and the Easter Bunny. I liked the stories of God I knew from childhood when they portrayed God as a kind, jovial, gift-giving God. As a teen, however, God became a lot less fun. God became a much more demanding, offended, and annoyed voyeur who was incessantly looking for ways to demonstrate his authority over me and the world.

When I was in seminary as a young adult, I regained a high regard for the Bible. This time, however, my regard for the Bible was about ideas, philosophy, and matters related to my existence and purpose as a human being. The Bible, for me, became valuable because of its existential reasoning and the arguments I could develop both for and against the various stories. In a sense, the Bible I had come to value again was merely a textbook on par with the other great works of literature and philosophy carefully aligned on my bookshelf. I valued the Bible, at this stage in my life, because of its rich and robust ideas and concepts. I doubted most of the Bible's teachings then, due to my inability to see their relevance for my life—or any human being's life.

I've learned over the years, however, that the Bible's value does not come from the prizes you are awarded as a kid, the use or abuse of it as a tool we hold over others' heads, or from use as a textbook. The Bible is a love story—the story of a loving, creative God who is good. It is a collection of wonderfully engaging stories, written in a variety of genres such as poetry, prophecy, and parables, meant not just to amuse or entertain, but to shape the very life we live.

The Bible is the story of the Hebrew people who were chosen and called to reveal God. The Hebrew people, as we see through the entirety of Scripture, struggled to remain faithful to God. God, in his immeasurable mercy, however, modeled to the Hebrew people through the life, death, burial, and resurrection of Jesus what it means to be a faithful revealer of God's goodness—and the many blessings that come from God.

When we engage the Bible through personal and group study or sermon, we encounter God. God has inspired the Bible, meaning that God has had an active role in shaping the Bible. The Bible is both divine and human. The Bible reveals the human struggle and, therefore, discloses all that is wrong with humanity—violence, lust, murder, injustice, paganism—and at the same time discloses God's enduring love that overcomes human deficiencies and provides new life.

I've learned over the years that engaging the Bible is more about intimacy, not literacy. Reading the Bible for knowledge of God is one thing. Allowing the Bible to read *you* for transformation is altogether different. Reading the Bible is important; allowing the Holy Spirit to guide us and teach us eternal truth is essential. When we allow the Bible to read us, we place ourselves under the authority of the Bible and allow its truth to shape our lives in intimate ways. The divine power of the Bible's truth (by the way, truth is a person and his name is Jesus) helps us to grow in our faith and allows us to gain insights into living holy and whole lives, the way God intended for us to live.

When we regularly engage the Bible, we carry to it all of our human experience—our joys, concerns, celebrations, and reasons for mourning. The Bible meets us head-on with God's promises of forgiveness and hope.

> **Today's Challenge**
>
> **Keep a Bible with you at all times today. Let it serve as a reminder of God's desire to be with you in every moment of your day. When you have a few free moments, use them to engage with Scripture.**

Wesley's question, "Did the Bible live in me today?" is profound. He didn't ask, "Did we read our Bible today?" but did it *live* in us. In other words, is the Bible actively shaping our heart, our inner self? It is critical for us that the Bible shapes our thinking, but it is also very important that it shapes our being. As the Bible shapes our being—as we experience spiritual transformation—our doing is also shaped. The Bible is about inspiring all that we are—our heads, hearts and hands.

To allow the Bible to live in us, we must be humble people, taking a posture of listening, learning, action, and service. These stories of God point humanity toward one main, key idea. This idea is simply this: God desires the world to be whole, just as God created it to be. The brokenness we see every day in our lives is not God's intention for this world. We move toward living whole lives and showing others what wholeness looks like when we let the Bible have influence in our lives and allow it to guide and direct us toward active participation with God's mission to restore the world toward its intended wholeness.

Reflection Questions

1. How do you let the Bible live in you each day?
2. Has your view of the Bible changed throughout your life? Do you value the Bible differently, or relate to it differently, than you did when you were younger?

Personal Application Ideas

1. Recall a Bible story you learned as a child (such as Noah's ark, or Samson and Delilah). Write down the key story elements as you remember them from that time. Try to recall your main understanding of the story.
2. Reread that story. You can find these stories in Scripture by using biblegateway.com's search feature. What elements of the narrative are you discovering that you didn't understand as a child? What are your primary takeaways from this story now? How has your life experience enriched your understanding of God's word?

scripture

"I am the true vine, and my Father is the vineyard keeper. He removes any of my branches that don't produce fruit, and he trims any branch that produces fruit so that it will produce even more fruit. You are already trimmed because of the word I have spoken to you. Remain in me, and I will remain in you. A branch can't produce fruit by itself, but must remain in the vine. Likewise, you can't produce fruit unless you remain in me. I am the vine; you are the branches. If you remain in me and I in you, then you will produce much fruit. Without me, you can't do anything. If you don't remain in me, you will be like a branch that is thrown out and dries up. Those branches are gathered up, thrown into a fire, and burned. If you remain in me and my words remain in you, ask for whatever you want and it will be done for you. My Father is glorified when you produce much fruit and in this way prove that you are my disciples."

John 15:1-8

Prayer

God, prepare my ears to hear your voice as I study your Word. Open my heart and mind to the truths that are held within its pages. Help me to discover clarity of thinking, being, and doing from your Word.

Holy Spirit, guide me into all truth and expand my understanding of the person and work of Jesus in a real and living way. Amen.

*God desires that we radiate
God's love and when we choose
to let brokenness, fear, or despair
rule the day, we do not live out
God's intended way of life.*

Chapter 5

DID I DISOBEY GOD IN ANYTHING?

When God created human beings God did so with complete love. God's love, demonstrated in the good creation of our world, however, was so intense and weighty that in it there resided at least two fundamental properties.

First, God's complete love gave humans complete freedom. God gave human beings the freedom to love God or not. To love God is to obey God; to disobey God is to love the self more than God. It might seem hard to imagine that a powerful, all-knowing God would create humans with such a personal power. God understood, however, that in order to love a person, there must be a real freedom for those God loves to love back or not. Love, to be genuine, must be mutual. God did not preprogram or hardwire humans with an obedience code. Humans are not robots that must behave as encoded, for that is not love—that is control. God created humans with the ability to choose, and humans make choices every day that place their love for God over love for self, or self over God.

As we know all too well, Adam and Eve (a representation for all people throughout history) usurped the authority of God by loving self above God and therefore disobeyed God by eating the fruit of the Tree of the Knowledge of Good and Evil. Adam and Eve's disobedience was a decision to love self above God, to try to be gods themselves. This, to this very day, is the enduring struggle of every human being. The question is: will we love self above God, or will we love God above self?

The second key property of God's love in the creation of humans is what is referred to as the possibility of sin. God knew that when granting liberty for humans to choose, that act was simultaneously creating the possibility for rebellion.

I am often asked if I believe God created sin. My answer is an emphatic, "No!" God did not create sin, but the possibility for sin was created when God gave humans the freedom to make their own decisions. I believe God created humans with goodness and the freedom to live into that goodness or choose otherwise. God's desire was for humans to love God with all of their heart, mind, soul, and strength, and in doing so worship God with all of life.

God is in pursuit of humanity, wooing us toward God's goodness each day. When we choose to obey God, we honor God's love for us, and we live the way that God desired for us to live. When we disobey God by choosing to live our own ways, we live into our freedom, yes, but we also live into the possibility of sin and make it a reality. I believe God has equipped humans, every one of us, with the ability to choose to do what is right or holy. Holiness is sometimes described as the radiance of God's glory. We do not choose to live holy or righteous lives for our own personal piety. On the contrary, we choose in complete freedom to live holy lives in order to reflect back onto God (and to the world around us) the glory of God, which radiates with complete love. This is what it means to be the light of the world—to shine God's goodness by choosing to obey God's desires.

I wish it were as easy to live obediently as it is to speak or write about it. To live holy or obedient lives is hard. It is hard because if it were not it wouldn't be a holy devotion to God, it would merely be a preprogrammed result. God wants us to love God back; therefore, we have complete freedom to choose. God's strong and unfailing desire is that we would love God back, but we often don't.

Sometimes we disobey God with the choices we make that bring us personal pleasure. At other times we disobey God by inappropriately demonstrating our power over people. Still, at other times in our lives, we inappropriately abuse our freedom when we lie, cheat, steal, or gossip. We disobey God every time we choose our own personal desires over God's desires.

We can also live into disobedience when we don't do the things God wants us to do. For example, God set the world up to be whole and unbroken. At those times that we do not stand for justice or speak up for the marginalized or those made to feel small, we also disobey God. Remember, God desires that we radiate God's love, and when we choose to let brokenness, fear, or despair rule the day, we do not live out God's intended way of life.

We do disobedient things, and we disobey God by not doing obedient things. So how do we move beyond a love for self and move to a whole-hearted love for God? It is simple, really (remember, simple doesn't always mean easy). When we do or don't do what God intends, we must choose to confess our actions (or lack of actions) and ask for forgiveness. We call this confession. When we are faithful to confess our shortcomings or when we miss the mark and tell God the truth, God meets our intermittent faithfulness with enduring faithfulness and grants us grace, which gives us the chance to begin again. Confession taps into God's forgiveness, and forgiveness gives us a fresh start. This is yet another example of God's great love for humans. God's love is always greater than your biggest blunder.

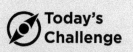 **Today's Challenge**

Sometime today spend a few minutes reflecting on your life. In what areas of your life are you intentionally living for your own self rather than for God's glory? After determining the area or areas of disobedience in your life, tell God you are sorry. Also, tell one of your Christian friends what you are struggling with so this person can offer you accountability, help, and support.

Reflection Questions

1. In what areas of my life am I choosing my own desires over God's desires?

2. Where can I find help in overcoming my shortcomings?
3. How can I use the freedom that God has granted me to worship God?

Personal Application Ideas

1. Memorize the following verse. "To you, LORD, belong greatness and power, honor, splendor, and majesty, because everything in heaven and on earth belongs to you. Yours, LORD, is the kingship, and you are honored as head of all" (1 Chronicles 29:11).
2. When you sense a struggle within you to usurp God's authority and behave out of your own personal desires, repeat the verse to yourself.
3. Text or e-mail three people right now and ask them to ask you the question, "Did I disobey God in anything?" at least once a week.
4. Reread Genesis chapters 1 and 2, and make a list of the ideas that point to God's goodness in the world and God's desire for humans to live them out.

---

scripture

You must walk the precise path that the LORD your God indicates for you so that you will live, and so that things will go well for you, and so you will extend your time on the land that you will possess.

Deuteronomy 5:33

Prayer

God, you gladly and graciously forgive all who repent of their sins and turn toward you. Thanks for your promise of enduring and redeeming grace! May we strive to be as Christ is, perfect in every way, in order that we might reveal our love for you to the world around us. Amen.

Chapter 6

DO I PRAY ABOUT THE MONEY I SPEND?

Jesus and John Wesley had much in common. One thing they had in common was that they both talked about money a lot. Money, one of the three biggies when it comes to human struggle (sex and power being the other two), makes people do funny things. Whether a person has great wealth, or no wealth to speak of, the money we possess, or wish we possessed, shapes how each one of us chooses to live.

Of course, money in itself is not inherently bad. We know from the Scriptures that it is the *love* of money that can sometimes lead us astray—away from a deeper relationship with God, self, and others. We are also taught in the Scriptures that we cannot serve both God and money. Serving God first means we choose to make money second place or even third or fourth place, in our lives. Choosing money over God means we place God second or third or fourth. It is really that simple. Money has the power to either help us become more deeply committed Christians or to hinder our efforts. This is why John Wesley puts forward the question, "Do I pray about the money I spend?"

It is widely known that Wesley said, "Gain all you can, save all you can, and give all you can." This is helpful advice and a great framework for how we can commit daily to putting God first in our lives, particularly as it relates to our relationship with money. It is important to remember that these three lessons from Wesley—gain, save, and give—should be kept in balance and harmony.

To gain all we can does not mean we make money at the expense of others. It does not mean that we gain in such a way as to impact our personal or family health. It does mean that the businesses we choose to create, run, and work for do not take away from God's kingdom ethics; instead, they should work to bring heaven to earth. To gain all that we can does not give us permission to lie, cheat, trick, or steal or mean we can dismiss Kingdom ethics.

To save all we can means, very simply, that as Christians working toward a deeper commitment to God and God's design of goodness or wholeness for the world, we avoid spending wantonly or carelessly for personal pleasure so that we can respond to the expected and unexpected needs of self and others. To save is not to look for a great bargain at your favorite department store. To save is not to negotiate the absolute best deal you can get on that new car you don't need but want. To save is to make sure that we are prepared for the curveballs life throws our way and that we do not let the indulgences of personal pleasure lead us away from a deeper union with God.

To give all we can means that we steward the money we gain and save in such a way that we are able to use it for God's work in this world. To give all we can clearly does not mean that we are to donate all of our money and in doing so neglect our personal and family responsibilities. We must give to God's work in the world with wisdom and with a deep sense of harmony. When we learn the importance of giving, we are able to see that the needs of others are as important as our own. This is what deeply committed Christians do; they learn to discover and uphold the other, whoever that may be, equal to self.

Jesus taught us a great deal about money as well. Jesus taught that money is important so that we can give to God's work, care for our families, and care for others. Jesus cautioned us not to store treasures up in barns, and he demonstrated on at least one occasion how he felt when money became the priority over God. This was when Jesus overturned the money changers' tables in the Jerusalem Temple as vendors took advantage of people on pilgrimage to worship. If Jesus were in our churches, our homes, and places of work and fun today, I'm quite sure that he would provoke our minds and hearts with a statement such as, "Followers of mine do not ask how much money they should give to God. On the contrary, people who follow me ask how much of God's money will I keep for myself and my family?"

Today's Challenge

Bless someone with your money today. Make the amount significant enough that it will feel like a sacrifice to you. Have the money ready in your pocket or purse so that you can act when the moment presents itself. Don't second-guess yourself. Act.

To pray about the money we spend means that we go to God realizing that we do not personally possess any money of our own. Rather, we are simply holding God's money for the purposes of God's work in the world—to provide the essentials for our families in order that we can work to feed the hungry, clothe the naked, provide shelter for the homeless, and, as far as our money will go, to make the world a place that looks like the kingdom of God.

This means that we take the time to reflect upon the gaining, saving, and giving of the money we hold, in order that we might continuously work to allow God to be first in our lives and that our pursuit of provisions is not based on our own abilities but on God's generosity.

Reflection Questions

1. What were your thoughts as you read Wesley's statement: "Gain all you can, save all you can, give all you can"? Were you surprised by any part of the quote?
2. How often do you pray about the money you spend? Do you pray before large purchases and donations only? What

might happen to your spending habits if you prayed daily about the money you spend?

Personal Application Ideas

1. Take a few moments to evaluate your recent spending. Do your habits fall in line with Wesley's advice? Why or why not? Make a chart with three columns: Gain, Save, and Give. In each column, estimate the amounts you have gained, saved, or given in the past year. What are your feelings as you review the past year's results? Are you moved to make any changes in your spending life?
2. At the beginning of each day, ask God for his guidance in your earning and spending habits for that day. Listen for his voice as you conduct yourself in business and as you consider purchases.

scripture

Then Jesus said to them, "Watch out! Guard yourself against all kinds of greed. After all, one's life isn't determined by one's possessions, even when someone is very wealthy.

Luke 12:15

Prayer

God, I want to be a sensible steward of all you have provided, and truthful in all my transactions using money. Protect me, God, from having an attitude marked by greed but rather may I grow toward a faithful generosity, combined with insight that only comes from you. Also, God, help me to spend whatever money you allow me to possess in a way that brings glory to you. Amen.

Chapter 7

DO I GIVE TIME FOR THE BIBLE TO SPEAK TO ME EVERY DAY?

A friend of mine told me, "Finding and then taking the time to read the Bible is just too difficult." He went on, "Most of the time I sit down to read my Bible I am quickly confused by it. I can never tell exactly how I am to understand it—or how it is somehow supposed to 'speak' to me."

This is a very common struggle for Christians. First, it's tough to find the time in our busy lives to read the Bible. Second, it isn't easy to take the time once we have found it. Finally, it can be a challenge to understand what we are reading once we have made the time to read the Bible. Fear not! There is a way to do this faithfully and successfully. Warning: It will require that you work at it. If you truly want to develop the discipline of Bible reading, this chapter can help you—but you'll have to commit. It will come—but not without some effort on your part.

Let's first understand what it means to have the Bible "speak" to us. This can seem mystical or even awkward and impossible for some. It is essential that we understand what the word *speak* means in the context of Bible reading. Here are three elements of our Christian faith that help us understand what it means to have the Bible "speak" to us:

- **Revelation**: God makes truth known by revealing it to us through the Bible. When we say God inspired the Bible, we mean God intentionally gave us the Bible by collaborating with human authors to help us know who God is and what God is like.
- **Illumination:** When God makes truth known, God also gives us understanding of the truth. The ministry of the Holy Spirit is to take truth from the Bible and allow us to comprehend it. Our minds and hearts are shaped when the Spirit lights up the Bible. Then it speaks to us.
- **Imagination:** God reveals truth to us, helps us to understand it, and then fires our imagination, giving us ways to live truth and share it with others. When God fires our imaginations, God helps us to internalize the truth and gives us opportunities to actively participate with God's work in the world.

God speaks to us through revelation and illumination and by firing our imagination. To allow God to speak to us through the Bible we must develop the discipline of regular Bible reading and study. The discipline of finding and taking the time is essential to growing in our Christian faith. Wesley asks this question not to create more for the Christian to do. Rather, Wesley makes us confront our efforts to engage the Bible as we seek to have God speak to us so that we might become more deeply committed Christians. Bible reading is not a task to be completed; it is a practice to shape us and mold us into who God invites us to be.

It is important to remember that we do not put our faith in the Bible. We put our faith in the God of the Bible. The God of the Bible wants us to develop the discipline of knowing, loving, and serving God more deeply through Bible reading. Here are four important attributes we must possess to develop the consistent practice of Bible reading and to allow God to speak to us:

- **Humility:** people who come to the Scriptures to listen, knowing they have more to learn, create a greater opportunity to have God speak to them.

- **Open-mindedness:** people who come to the Scriptures to find new truth create a greater opportunity to have God speak to them.
- **Obedience:** people who come to the Scriptures willing to take action, or put into practice what they learn, create a greater opportunity for God to speak to them.
- **Determination:** people who resolve to find the time, taking the time and desiring to understand what they are reading and learning as truth, create a greater opportunity to have God speak to them.

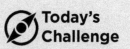 **Today's Challenge**

Devote twenty minutes to reading one of the Gospels today. Approach the time with an open mind and heart. Listen for God's voice as you read and reflect. What did you hear?

God wants to communicate love to us. God does this in many ways—through creation, through our conscience, and through the life of Christ. These ways, coupled with the Bible, help us hear God speak. God may speak through other means like music, prayer, or circumstances. Learning to listen to God through the Bible, I believe, helps us become more aware of other ways in which God desires to speak to us.

Reflection Questions

1. Do you struggle with finding the time or taking the time to read the Bible each day? Or is your challenge more about understanding and interpreting what you've read?
2. How has God spoken to you through the Bible? Has God spoken to you in a different way, such as music or prayer, or through another person?

Personal Application Ideas

1. If you know someone who has developed the discipline of daily Bible reading, ask about his or her routine and experiences. See if a similar approach might help you

become better able to listen for God speaking through the Bible to you.

2. Sign up to have a daily devotional sent to your phone or e-mail. Start your day by reading that devotional and giving yourself time to process its meaning for you.

---

scripture

God's word is living, active, and sharper than any two-edged sword. It penetrates to the point that it separates the soul from the spirit and the joints from the marrow. It's able to judge the heart's thoughts and intentions.

Hebrews 4:12

Prayer

God, stir within me a passion to read your Scriptures and to regularly meditate on them throughout the days and weeks. I ask that you grant me the ability to understand what I need to put your teachings into practice. Help me to remember that good intentions are worthless, unless connected to and rooted in your love and grace. Help the words of the Bible not to be just words on a page, but passageways of mercy into my heart. Amen.

Section 2

RELATIONSHIP WITH SELF: AN INWARD FOCUS

Section 2

RELATIONSHIP WITH SELF: AN INWARD FOCUS

Authentic followers of Jesus take the time to inspect their interior lives. Christians who seek to inspect their interior lives know that in order to most faithfully and effectively participate in God's mission, they must be healthily self-aware. Christians who are self-aware are those who do the hard work of introspection in order to mature and grow in their faith.

Healthy, self-aware Christians are people who can look deep into their soul, reflect upon the truth and who they are truthfully becoming, and, as a result of that realization, make the necessary changes to become who God created them to be.

Wesley knew that in order to fully live into our God-intended design, we must be authentic people whose inner lives match our outer lives. Wesley gave us seven questions that lead us toward determining our true self. In order to be real and true to our emerging faith, Christians must do the hard work of becoming honest with themselves.

In becoming honest with our true selves it is important to remember that God loves us as we are. We do not need to beat ourselves up, knowing that we have weaknesses and shortcomings.

Instead, because we know our value and worth in God's eyes, we seek to become the people God intends for us to be. We do not earn God's love; it is freely given to us. Sometimes the hardest person for us to love is our own self.

Do not spend the next few days of reading, reflection, and challenge assessing your interior life only to become disheartened or discouraged. Instead, do the hard work of discovering who you really are but then know that God loves you just as you are! Yes, God is jealous for our attention, love, and focus, and, yes, we should continually seek to live what God intends for us. However, the last thing God wants is for you to feel sadness or sorrow. God wants you to find and experience the peace and joy that comes from knowing you are loved.

Self-reflection for the purpose of realizing your true self is hard work. Resist the temptation to move past it quickly and not truly search, but at the same time resist the temptation to become defeated. Wesley's questions are meant to help us become who God intends for us to be. They are not intended to make us into people who are overwhelmed or conquered by self-hate and, therefore, unable to see our capability of a total love for God and others.

Chapter 8

AM I PROUD?

Contributed by Chris Abel

On February 14, 1990, the Voyager 1 space probe took a photo of Earth from 3.7 billion miles away. Our entire planet fits inside a single pixel of this photograph. The photo, requested by Carl Sagan, was used in his public lecture where he said these now famous words:

> That's here. That's home. That's us. On it, everyone you ever heard of, every human being who ever lived, lived out their lives. The aggregate of all our joys and sufferings, thousands of confident religions, ideologies and economic doctrines, every hunter and forager, every hero and coward, every creator and destroyer of civilizations, every king and peasant, every young couple in love, every hopeful child, every mother and father, every inventor and explorer, every teacher of morals, every corrupt politician, every superstar, every supreme leader, every saint and sinner in the history of our species, lived there—on a mote of dust, suspended in a sunbeam....It has been said that astronomy is a humbling and character-building experience. There is

perhaps no better demonstration of the folly of human conceits than this distant image of our tiny world. To me, it underscores our responsibility to deal more kindly with one another, and to preserve and cherish the pale blue dot, the only home we've ever known.[1]

You and I live on this "pale blue dot," as Sagan called it. But unlike the Voyager 1 space probe, we don't have access to this perspective. We don't have the privilege to see our lives from the far reaches of space. We live very much on the surface of that dot. We live our one human life, eyes close to the ground, caught up in our day-to-day busyness. And from that perspective, the small things often feel like big things, don't they?

And a strange phenomenon happens when we live on the surface of that pale blue dot. Even though we're a small part of something big, there's a temptation to think highly of ourselves. We all know those people who walk around as if they were puffed up with air, proud of their bank account statement, their title, their looks, their ability. Sometimes, *we're* even those people!

Saint Augustine once said that pride is "the love of one's own excellence." This goes beyond simply healthy self-esteem. This is a perspective that says we are somehow superior. For instance, let's say a man is really good at making cheese. Even the most lactose-intolerant person knows that cheese is amazing. And this man's cheese is top-notch. He knows it. But the moment his cheese-making makes him feel *better* than other people is the moment he has found his identity in cheese. As a speck of dust in all the universe, this man somehow feels superior *about cheese*.

It's a ridiculous analogy—because pride is ridiculous. Being prideful about your cheese-making ability is a strange thing to feel superior about. But we all do this. It may not be cheese, but we take little parts of our lives and feel superior about them. If it's not making cheese, it's our intellect. If it's not our intellect, it's our looks. If it's not our looks, it's our possessions. If it's not our possessions, it's our freedom from material possessions. We can literally be prideful about *anything*. Here's why it is so important to reflect on this:

Pride is a symptom that your perspective is too close to the earth.

When your heart and soul are face down toward your own life, you will naturally struggle with pride. When your energy and time and thoughts all revolve around your life, concerns, and pleasures, you will absolutely feel superior. You are, after all, living as if you're the center of the universe.

But when we look at the earth as a pale blue dot, everything is cheese-making.

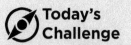

Today's Challenge

Ask a trusted friend or mentor to share their opinion of your three biggest strengths and three biggest areas of improvement.

God, luckily for us, isn't bound by gravity. God doesn't see things from our limited, vertically challenged perspective. The God of the universe sees us as we are: limited and beautiful. Flawed yet full of amazing potential.

Jesus once had a conversation with a Jewish teacher named Nicodemus. Nicodemus had every right to be proud. He was a very respected cheese-maker/teacher. And yet he was curious about Jesus' teachings. And so Jesus said to him, "I assure you, unless someone is born anew, it's not possible to see God's kingdom" (John 3:3). My Bible has an asterisk near that word *anew* that says "or *from above*." In Greek, these are the same word: *anew* and *above*. Often this story gets understood as Jesus saying "born again," a phrase popular in evangelical circles. But *above* actually fits better. "I assure you, unless someone is born (*from above*), it's not possible to see God's kingdom."

When you're too close to the ground, you can't see the Kingdom. Jesus teaches us to live our lives from *above*. Just like seeing a city from an airplane, when we are born from above, we get a different perspective on what God is doing in the world. When we have a higher perspective, it's hard to feel pride about something so small, isn't it?

Many psychologists theorize that pride, ironically, is a symptom of low self-esteem. When we don't feel secure, we find security and acceptance in any area of life we can. Pride is a problem, but it is intricately tied with feelings of insecurity and worthlessness. When we ask ourselves "Am I proud?" we are also asking ourselves "am I secure in my identity?"

This is nothing new. Rabbi Simcha Bunam, who taught hundreds of years ago, was known to have two slips of paper on him at all times, one in each pocket. On the first piece of paper he wrote "For my sake was the world created." On the other he wrote, "I am earth and ashes."[2]

You are just a speck on a speck in a massive universe. But it's equally true that you are beautifully and wonderfully made. As the psalmist writes to God, "You are the one who created my innermost parts; / you knit me together while I was still in my mother's womb. / I give thanks to you that I was marvelously set apart. / Your works are wonderful—I know that very well" (Psalm 139:13-14).

So take comfort in the fact that you are valuable and precious to God. But so is everyone else. We're all blessed with life, and we all have gifts. Don't let pride keep you from seeing our world like God sees our world—a beautiful, special, loved, pale blue dot.

Reflection Questions

1. Where in my life do I mask insecurities with pride?
2. What are my strengths from God's perspective?
3. What will I leave behind in one thousand years?

Personal Application Ideas

1. Find time to pray at night under the stars.
2. Google "AMNH Known Universe" and watch a video on the size of the universe.

scripture

You are the one who created my innermost parts;
　you knit me together while I was still in my mother's womb.
I give thanks to you that I was marvelously set apart.
　Your works are wonderful—I know that very well.

Psalm 139:13-14

Prayer

Creator of the universe, we thank you for the gift of life you've entrusted in us. Guard our hearts and attitudes that we may see as you see. Help us find security in you and free us from the need to feel superior. Let us see our place in your Kingdom and humble ourselves before our brothers and sisters. Amen.

A strong person admits the need for help and calls out for it. We are not a failure because we are failing at something. Our strength does not reside in our own self. Our strength comes from God, the source of all of strength and life itself.

Chapter 9

AM I DEFEATED IN ANY PART OF MY LIFE?

A few weeks ago I went to a local health-care facility to visit someone I know. He was in a mental health center that specializes in caring for people who have had or are experiencing acute depression.

When his wife called me to tell me that he had attempted suicide and was admitted to the facility, I was completely caught off guard. I was shocked, actually. Every time I saw him—at the gym, at church, at the ball fields, at a restaurant, I would ask him what I typically ask everyone I come into contact with: "How are you doing?" His response was always something like, "I am doing great. Life couldn't be better." He would use different words each time to describe how he was doing, but his response was always similar to that—and so upbeat and emphatic too. Clearly, my friend wasn't doing great, and life could definitely have been better.

The simple truth is this—we all have points in our life when we feel defeated or overcome with emotions or feelings or stress or pressure that, if not dealt with, can wreak havoc on our mental, physical, emotional, and spiritual health. I am as guilty as my friend when it comes to creating the illusion that I am doing better than I really am. My guess is that you can also point to times in your life when you are in need of rest, relaxation, or recreation. It is OK to be defeated or overcome with the stressors of life. This does not make you any less of a person.

We are designed to be in community. We are most fully human when we are in authentic, trusting relationships with others. We are meant to live life with the help, encouragement, and support of others. God has given us a great gift—the gift of other people to surround us, build us up and give us the inspiration we need to live healthy lives.

While it isn't very common to have someone respond to "How are you doing?" with anything other than a positive response, we must work to create the kind of community that allows people to be truthful. We must be the kind of friend, spouse, or coworker who creates an environment for people to say, "I am not doing so well, actually. I could use some help." (By the way, don't ask the "How are you doing?" question unless you are actually willing to listen intently to the other person's story and willing to be used by God to provide support.)

Why is it so hard for us to be honest? More often than not, we feel we need to put on a mask or to create a front that makes everything seem OK even when it isn't. For some it might be the desire not to appear weak. For others it might be that the admission of failing at anything means they are a failure. This, of course, is not the case. A strong person admits the need for help and calls out for it. We are not a failure because we are failing at something. Our strength does not reside in our own self. Our strength comes from God, the source of all of strength and life itself.

To admit that we are defeated is an act of courage. To admit that we need help is bravery. To admit that our stability, strength, and sustainability come from God is an act of worship. We honor God when we declare our need for God's help. The Psalms are filled with constant cries for help and support.

Typically, when I feel myself feeling defeated, it has to do with poor eating habits, lack of exercise, not enough sleep or rest, neglecting my daily prayer and Bible reading, and the like. Often I am unable to climb out of my funk because I put my hope and strength in my own skills and abilities. This is a form of conceit. To think I don't need help to overcome the obstacles I might be facing is arrogant and self-loving. The help I often need is a friend to come alongside me to remind me of the important things I am missing.

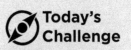

Today's Challenge

Admit to the people closest to you that you are feeling defeated. Be specific. If you are not feeling defeated at the moment, your challenge is to share with a friend the areas in your life in which you most often feel defeated and why.

Again, it is OK to feel defeated. However, God desires that we live joyful lives. God desires that our joy be found in God's goodness and gifts of life. God grants us gifts like grace, mercy, forgiveness, hope, faithfulness, and peace. To experience these gifts fully we need to place our full trust and faith in God's strength, not in our own. When you feel defeated you must admit it, surround yourself with people who love you and can live into God's gifts to support you. It is important to understand that our trust and faith, or lack thereof, does not diminish God. Our lack of trust and faith and the other elements of our life that can defeat us do, however, diminish our ability to experience God's gifts.

Reflection Questions

1. In what areas of my life do I often feel defeated? *MOST CHALLENGED: CAREER RELATED PEOPLE/LEADERS*
2. Is there anything in my life that I could change, such as *YES - ENFORCE* personal habits like eating healthier or exercising more, that would help me overcome feeling defeated?
3. What are the warning signs in my life that help me see my need for help and support? *SIGNS OF PHYSICALLY STRESSED*

Personal Application Ideas

1. Make a list of as many of God's traits, such as strength, goodness, and so on as you can think of. Use this list to remind you where your strength comes from.

2. Ask a friend to monitor the warning signs in your life (the ones you reflected on above) and to be honest with you when you display them.
3. Read this verse every day for the next week to remind yourself where your strength to overcome comes from:

> The Lord is my solid rock,
>   my fortress, my rescuer.
> My God is my rock—
> I take refuge in him! —
>   he's my shield,
>   my salvation's strength,
>   my place of safety.
>   (Psalm 18:2)

---

scripture

I've said these things to you so that you will have peace in me. In the world you have distress. But be encouraged! I have conquered the world.

John 16:33

Prayer

God, we ask you to exchange victory for defeat. Help all of us who feel defeated to center our thoughts on the many blessings in our lives instead of our current or past circumstances. We ask you, God, that you grow our hope with great joy. Amen.

Chapter 10

DO I GO TO BED ON TIME
AND GET UP ON TIME?

I used to have incredibly poor sleeping habits. The older I get, however, the more I have come to appreciate what a good night's sleep brings. We all know what it feels like to wake up feeling refreshed and alert. Sleep is critical to our spiritual and physical health and wellness.

Of course, like any other healthy habit, getting to bed on time and getting up on time requires discipline. Wesley's question, "Do I go to bed on time and get up on time?" is about being rested for the work of God in the world, yes. However, his question also points to our willingness to live a disciplined life in general.

We all know the benefits of being rested. Some of these include being more joyful the next day, having a clearer mind or sharper memory, driving more safely, making better decisions, and experiencing an overall optimistic outlook on life.

If there are benefits or advantages to sleep, then there are corresponding disadvantages to not getting enough sleep. I would venture to say that almost every one of you reading these words has had a time or two in your life when you, for whatever reason, have not been able to get enough sleep. Just as you know the advantages, you have, at one time or another, come face to face with the disadvantages. When I don't go to bed on time and wake up on time, I am grumpy, my mind is cluttered, I am lethargic and sluggish, and I walk around like I am in a fog. This means I am missing opportunities to participate in God's mission to restore the world toward its intended wholeness.

I think if Wesley were alive today and proposing this question, he would help us see that it isn't just about going to bed on time and getting up on time. I think he would help us wrestle with what it means to be in good health (spiritually, physically, socially, financially) overall.

In Mark 1:29-39, we see Jesus engaged in God's work of healing sick people. The Scriptures indicate that "the whole town" gathered at the door of the house where Jesus was staying, and throughout the night Jesus healed many. After Jesus had healed many, we see him choosing to find a solitary place where he could be renewed. Mark 1:35 says, "Early in the morning, well before sunrise, Jesus rose and went to a deserted place where he could be alone in prayer. To be in good health may not only require a full night's rest—it may also require times of solitude.

Jesus knew the importance of finding the time to be renewed in order that he might remain focused on the mission at hand. After his disciples had gone looking for Jesus and found him praying in seclusion (1:36-37), Jesus led them to the next place of ministry in Galilee, where he could engage the people of that town and continue God's work. Can you imagine what it would have been like to heal people all night long and then depart for the next village to do the same thing without being rested? It is very likely you *do* know what that feels like. Perhaps you are a teacher who spends your day and night giving your time and energy to the development of students. Maybe you are a salesperson constantly on the road selling a product or service, and you jet all over the world doing the same thing day after day. I am sure some of you reading this are in the construction business, in health care, or in a service industry of some kind. What do you feel like when you are not rested enough to do your job? This is what Wesley wants us to face head-on. What do we need to do to be our best? What do we need to do to stay healthy so that whatever our profession might be, we do it faithfully and we do it knowing that as Christians we represent more than our company or ourselves? We represent God, and by working hard we bring honor to God. When we are rested and at our best, we can be sure to find ways to participate in God's mission while we are working.

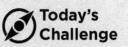

Today's Challenge

Like the flight attendant mentioned in this chapter, be determined to make the world a better place for the people you come in contact with today. Challenge yourself to make people feel better about themselves because of you.

I was on a flight a few weeks ago from Denver to Kansas City. All of the flight attendants were great. One woman in particular was exceptional. The minute I walked on the plane and she greeted me, I felt a warmth that I don't often feel on flights. Because of her desire to create an environment of hospitality, she was uplifting. She turned my mundane day into a great day. As I was deplaning, I thanked her and remarked, "You are great at your job. You must really love it." She responded by saying, "My job is hard. People can be mean. I have found if I rise above the negativity and create a place where people feel better about themselves and their experience on this flight, I can make the world a better place."

This is what Wesley wants us to realize, that by asking us this simple question. "Do we go to bed on time and get up on time?" it is code for "Are you rested and at your best so that you can meet the challenges of the day and ultimately help make the world a better place?"

Reflection Questions

1. How would you answer this question of John Wesley's, both on the surface level (adequate hours of sleep) and on its deeper level (rested enough to make the world a better place)?

NIGHT BEFORE FELL ASLEEP IN CHAIR DOING HOME WORK.

2. Think about a time you've felt exhausted and depleted. What was your behavior like at that time? What kind of decisions did you make when you were in that state?

Personal Applications

1. Choose a reasonable bedtime this week, one that will provide you with a good amount of rest, and stick to it. Perhaps it's a half hour before you usually go to bed, or perhaps it's a lot sooner than that. Don't allow e-mails, television, or anything else that can wait until the next day to interfere with that time you've set.
2. Incorporate one additional healthy habit into your day. Start small so that you will stick with it. Perhaps it's replacing an afternoon soda with ice water, or taking your dog on a ten-minute walk after work. Add something to your day to help you feel renewed.

---

scripture

On the sixth day God completed all the work that he had done, and on the seventh day God rested from all the work that he had done. God blessed the seventh day and made it holy, because on it God rested from all the work of creation.

Genesis 2:2-3

Prayer

God, help me to be disciplined in my sleep and in my times of rest and recreation. Help me to be fully rested so that as my feet hit the floor in the morning, whatever time that may be, I am refreshed and ready to do your work in the world. I pray, Oh, God, that I would be willing to stick to a schedule that allows me to be my best for your Kingdom's sake. Amen.

Chapter 11

DO I GRUMBLE OR COMPLAIN CONSTANTLY?

We all know that one person in our family, friend group, or workplace who always seems to be complaining about something. Typically, these people always seem to be grumbling due to a number of factors. First, they grumble because dwelling on the negative is easier than doing the hard work of fixing what might be broken. Second, people complain because they want to pass on the responsibility to somebody else. They want to avoid being seen as part of the problem but are often unwilling to take up progress toward a solution. Third, people can be heard constantly griping because they feel as though something that needs to change is out of their personal control. This creates a false sense of reality, and the negativity they embrace just compounds and makes for more negativity.

To be honest, I think people complain because they haven't yet discovered what it means to be content. People who complain, who are not content with life, are not able to live at peace with themselves and typically blame everyone else for their circumstances or situation. When we learn to be content or satisfied, we reverse the patterns of negativity in our life and find the positive. This changes our outlook from "doom and gloom" to "room to bloom." People who have an optimistic outlook on life, who avoid complaining, see the room in life, the potential for things to blossom and flourish.

Don't know if you are a complainer? Ask the people around you. We all complain about something at times, but the constant complainer usually gives off destructive vibes and, therefore, is someone to be avoided. I know a person (not very well, I admit, because I don't want their negative vibes to rub off on me) who is a constant complainer. The food is always bad, the service is always poor, the boss is always wrong, the music is always off, the day is always long, the temperature is either too hot or too cold, the grass is always greener, their coworkers are always not pulling their weight, the sky is always falling...you get the point. Sometimes I'm tempted to say, "Blah, blah, blah...shut up!" Am I right?

The Israelites were constantly complaining when Moses was leading them during the years of wandering. The Book of Numbers says God was so sick and tired of hearing their complaints that he burned the outer edges of their camp! Can you blame God? Seriously, constant complainers do nothing but drag others down. God has freed them from slavery! Yet they say they'd like to return to the land where they were held captive because it gave them what they wanted: lush green landscape with all the fish and meat they could eat. Did they really want to go back into slavery? Probably not, but they said they did in the moment because they were discontented. Their selfish personal desires superseded their memory of God's deliverance from bondage.

People who complain think they are merely making observations and stating reality. In actuality, complainers are creating an alternative reality that leads them to shirk responsibility and blame others for their discontentedness.

Complainers are not necessarily bad people. Often they just need an attitude adjustment so instead of seeing what is wrong with the world they find ways to reveal God's love in constructive and affirming ways, making the world right or good.

Let's play out this fictitious scenario: A friend of yours who is a constant complainer has, as long as you have known the person, said things like, "My church is boring," "The music at my church is not good," "My pastor's sermons are too long," "It is a pain to find a parking spot at my church," "My church is so big it is hard to make friends" or "My church is too small—everyone knows too much about each other." Easter, Christmas, or some special church event rolls around, and the complainer decides to take up the pastor's challenge to invite nonreligious friends. So the complainer says to a coworker, "My church is hosting a special event. You want to come with me?" Who in their right mind would want to come to this person's church after hearing nothing but complaints about it?

Wesley wanted his groups of disciples to ask one another this question, and us to ask ourselves and one another so that we can become aware of unintentional patterns or habits we might have formed. We ask this question of ourselves and one another in order to replace our negative thoughts with positive thoughts and start developing a new habit marked by hope and optimism.

Today's Challenge

Pay attention to your urge to complain throughout the day. When you find yourself on the verge of grumbling, stop. Ask yourself what would be gained by your complaining, and conversely, what might be lost by your complaining. Keep a mental note of how many times you were tempted to grumble about something. What does this tell you about yourself?

What's more, we need to ask this question to take responsibility for our role in the situations and circumstances that come our way and step up to participate in God's work cheerfully and with joy.

Choosing joy can be hard, no doubt. But this is what Christians are called to do. When we choose joy, we deflect the negativity that often paralyzes us and in its place reflect something greater. The good news is good for a reason. Let's be people who seek to choose joy over misery and reveal the good news through our contentment and gratitude for Jesus' saving work.

Reflection Questions

1. Do you think you are optimistic or pessimistic by nature? What kind of feedback have you received from people in your life about this aspect of your personality?

2. Do you think it is possible to reframe your approach to circumstances to view them in a positive versus negative light? What could help you do this?

Personal Application Ideas

1. Ask a trusted person in your life to tell you honestly if he or she views you as a complainer. Hopefully, the answer will be no, but if it is a yes, ask the person for an example and be willing to listen with an open heart and mind to the person's answer.
2. If you know a constant grumbler, commit to spending more time with the person (as much as is not toxic) to help you understand what might be driving the person's negative outlook. How can you help the reframe his or her outlook? What is the person missing in his or her life that you might help the person gain?

scripture

Do everything without grumbling and arguing so that you may be blameless and pure, innocent children of God surrounded by people who are crooked and corrupt. Among these people you shine like stars in the world because you hold on to the word of life. This will allow me to say on the day of Christ that I haven't run for nothing or worked for nothing.

Philippians 2:14-16

Prayer

Holy God, I praise you, for you are high and lifted up. You are worthy of all the praise, only you alone. I come before you knowing you are a God of grace and mercy. I give you thanks for all that I have—every test, every triumph, and every provision. You, God, always work for my good. May I honor you by avoiding complaining and replacing it with rejoicing even when things do not go my way.

Chapter 12

AM I A SLAVE TO DRESS, FRIENDS, WORK, OR HABITS?

I believe the underlying principle behind this question of Wesley's is simply: Who or what owns us? What consumes us? Who or what do we allow to control our lives?

When we are a slave to something or someone, it means that we take our direction from a controlling person or object that is not God. This submission to forces such as materialism, money, prestige, or fame gives us a false sense of freedom.

Let me illustrate this. There are some men who collect cars—a lot of cars. Some of them own dozens of sports cars and rare exotic cars and motorcycles too. There is nothing wrong with owning and collecting cars. But some men are absolutely consumed by these cars. Their entire week, when they are not at work making money to afford the cars, is spent in the garages polishing the cars—cars they do not even drive. There might be nothing wrong with this, except when their accountability as husband, dad, brother, and friend deteriorates because of this obsession with cars. They spend so much time with their cars, and away from their families, that their relationships falter.

While this illustration might seem extreme to many, it proves the point Wesley wants us to realize with his question. When we are slaves to dress, friends, work, habits, or any other controlling factor, we cannot faithfully live into deeper levels of union with God. Instead we allow ourselves to love earthly matters, which leads us into a deeper love for what pleases us rather than what pleases God.

Sometimes, it isn't about material possessions like cars. Rather, it is about a willingness to do whatever it takes to succeed or be seen as successful. This might show itself when we work long hours to build a name for ourselves or to prove to others that we are important and influential. For some, it isn't about importance and influence—it is about money or the need to feel secure. This need to feel secure can consume us, and in pursuing the feeling, we can become a slave to the idea of a secure and safe life. Rather than focus our attention on becoming more deeply committed Christians, we steer away toward selfish desires.

The fundamental inner battle each of us faces as a Christian is the battle between giving ourselves over to God's mission or living a life based on our own mission. When we are slaves to fashion, technology, people's opinions, or work, we cannot honestly turn ourselves over to be used for the mission of God in the world, which is to restore the world toward its intended wholeness.

People ask me all the time, "How do I know I am living in God's will?" My answer is always the same. When we give ourselves completely to the mission of God in the world, we are living in God's will. God's will is that the world would be whole. God's way of making the world whole is through the message of salvation and justice as known through the death, burial, and resurrection of Jesus. God's work in the world is carried on through the church. We cannot carry out God's work in the world when we are driven and consumed by material possessions or immaterial obsessions.

Here are three ways to help all of us intentionally choose to live according to God's mission rather than for the mission or desires of our own self:

1. **Observe and record your impulses.** When you feel yourself being pulled toward a certain vice such as shopping, overeating, working, or something else, be sure to notice the pull and record it. Recording it gives you a chance to look back and observe what pulls you and when. Then, as you understand the source, you can more effectively avoid the tug toward the vice. This allows you to keep the right priorities and focus on Kingdom living.

2. **Find a place to serve.** One of the best ways to control or curb your enthusiasm for anything other than God's mission that consumes you is to consistently serve others. Find a place where you can focus on others and their needs instead of your own desires. Attending to others tends to put our priorities in the right order.

3. **Think people over possessions.** We know that people matter more than the things we own. However, at times, our priorities get out of whack, and we can value some possession(s) over people. When we do this (either intentionally or unintentionally) we forget what really matters—people—and we work against God's good order for the world, which is whole, healthy, sustainable relationships.

Today's Challenge

Pay attention today to the messages you receive from your social media feeds, from your entertainment sources, and from the circle of your closest friends and acquaintances. Note how these messages might be influencing you to place possessions or other obsessions ahead of what God desires for you.

First in our life should be the intentions that God desires. We are called out of being slaves to what keeps us from loving God and loving others. We are called toward a healthy, balanced life of serving the Kingdom virtues we see in the life of Christ.

Reflection Questions

1. What controls your life? Be honest with yourself. What is the focus of most of your thoughts? What preoccupies you? How much time, effort, and focus would be available for your participation in the mission of God if this factor did *not* preoccupy your life?

2. Do you know someone who is noticeably enslaved by possessions or obsessions? What effect is this having on that person's life or their family's life?

Personal Application Ideas

1. Identify one preoccupation that holds you in its thrall. Perhaps it's the accumulation of material items. Perhaps it's your physical appearance. Tell your spouse or a trusted friend. Ask to be alerted when the person notices you "feeding" this preoccupation in any way. Commit to taking the person's feedback gracefully.

2. Find a place to serve regularly to help rebalance the priorities in your life. Don't put it off, and don't wait for the ideal service situation to present itself. Try out a variety of service opportunities to find the place that captures your attention and focus.

---

scripture

We didn't bring anything into the world and so we can't take anything out of it: we'll be happy with food and clothing. But people who are trying to get rich fall into temptation. They are trapped by many stupid and harmful passions that plunge people into ruin and destruction.

I Timothy 6:7-9

Prayer

God, help me to resist the desire to collect things I do not need. Help me also to resist the temptation to allow my impulses and obsessions to direct my decision-making and goal setting. Help me, God, to give you all I am and have. Amen.

Chapter 13

HOW DO I SPEND MY SPARE TIME?

I came across a recent study of Americans ages twenty-five to fifty-four, outlining the average workday of employed people with children under eighteen.[1] Here are some of the results of the study:

- Work and work-related activities: 8.9 hours
- Sleeping: 7.7 hours
- Eating and drinking: 1 hour
- Caring for others: 1.2 hour
- Household activities: 1 hour
- Leisure and sports: 2.5 hours
- Other: 1.6 hours

That's 16.3 hours awake and active. So what are we doing with our time? Clearly the average American who works and has kids under the age of eighteen is busy. Busy doing what? Well, some of the busyness comes from the necessary elements of parenting such as caring for others (I'm thinking of getting kids ready for school, making breakfast) and household activities (I'm thinking of things such as cleaning and driving kids to practice and extracurricular activities) and, of course, working in order to pay for it all. Americans are busy. However, in this 16.3-hour day, the average American who works and has kids under eighteen has 2.5 hours of leisure time, or what we might assume Wesley meant by spare time. So how are we using our spare time?

It is important to note that the 2.5 hours of spare time may not be a connected chunk of time or consecutive minutes during the day. Those 2.5 hours may be mixed into the other 16.3 and it may actually be difficult to find the spare time. Just because the study shows 2.5 hours of spare time in a pie chart doesn't mean it is easy to spot during the normal workday. This means that one of the most important elements to determining how you *spend* your spare time is to take notice and make observations as to when you actually *have* spare time.

For example, I usually get up between 6 and 6:30 a.m. during the week. Sometimes my wife is already out the door for work. If my wife isn't already out the door by the time I get up, we typically tag team in the breakfast-making, lunch-packing, and driving the kids to school. We usually have our boys out the door by 7:10 to 7:15 a.m. Since my daughter drives herself to school, once I drop my boys off, I typically have forty-five minutes or so to get myself ready to get on my way to wherever my first meeting of the day is. I try not to schedule meetings prior to 8:30 a.m., so this allows me roughly an hour for what we might call spare time. If I do not build this time and protect it, I find that I run from meeting to meeting or conversation to conversation until late into the evening. I not only have to find where my spare time is; I must protect that time.

In addition to the approximate hour or so of spare time I have in the morning, I also work to find another hour in the later afternoon to protect as spare time. For me, these two hours are essential to re-create myself. I realize that your schedule is likely different. While we all have twenty-four hours, our work and other family activities are never the same. Therefore, your spare time will likely be at different times during the day. I also realize that your amount of time may vary from day to day. Some days you might get two hours, some days only one, and still other days you may end up with bonus time. It is essential to determine where in your day you have spare time.

In addition to determining where you have time, you must also find what you should *do* with your time. This is not a time set apart to answer e-mails you didn't get to during your 8.9 hours of work. Instead, this time should be used for you to re-create yourself. I believe Wesley is proposing this as a key question for Christians to ask of ourselves and one another so that we can determine which activities help us to be refreshed, renewed, and refocused on the essential priorities of our lives.

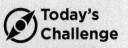

Today's Challenge

As your day unfolds, pay attention to your periods of spare time, and also how you fill that time. Record that information— honestly—and review it at the end of the day. Did you have more or less spare time than you anticipated? How do you feel about how you spent that time?

I use my spare time to exercise, read, write, drink a great cup of coffee, watch TED talks, pray, or hang out at my third place. (A "third place," by the way, is not home and is not work. A third place is where you can connect with self and others—the gym, a coffee shop, a pub, or a restaurant.)

These practices allow me to have some downtime and at the same time provide me with some "up" time. If used properly, spare time, as Wesley calls it in his question, can help us relax and at the same time gain the strength we need for whatever challenges, situations, and events (regardless of how mundane they may be) we face in our lives.

Along with the two hours of spare time I try and carve out each day, I also take three to five minutes three times a day to pray morning, midday, and evening prayers. As I mentioned in chapter 2, I've found a mobile app to be helpful in this prayer time. I don't get to these prayers every time every day. However, in addition to my spare time, I have found these prayer minutes to be a time for me to center myself on what is really important.

So, then, what is essential? First, determine in your day (workdays in particular) where your spare time might be. Second, once you determine your spare time, protect it and make it a priority. Finally, once you have established where your spare time is and protected it, determine the activities that help center you or help you re-create yourself. I don't think Wesley (or Jesus, for that matter) cares how we spend our spare time, as long as it enriches our lives and maybe even the lives of others around us. Wesley (and Jesus) both want to make sure that we are not wasting time, especially when we could be using it to strengthen our daily pursuit of becoming deeply committed Christians.

Reflection Questions

1. What activities bring you the most enjoyment and make you feel the most refreshed and energized?
2. How much of your spare time do you spend engaged in these pursuits? If it's less than you would like, how can you restructure your time so that you are spending it in ways that bring you life?

Personal Application Ideas

1. Make a spare-time map of your week. For one week, record everything honestly, just to be reviewed by you. Be specific enough so that you can spot spare-time patterns to help you evaluate your map. Use the calendar or notes functions on your phone to help you, or jot down notes in your desk calendar or portfolio, if that works best for you.
2. Choose one activity that renews you and brings you joy, and commit to including it in your spare time as often as is feasible (running might be doable most days, but rock-climbing or golfing might be more of a weekend activity).

scripture

Brothers and sisters, we command you in the name of our Lord Jesus Christ to stay away from every brother or sister who lives an undisciplined life that is not in line with the traditions that you received from us. You yourselves know how you need to imitate us because we were not undisciplined when we were with you. We didn't eat anyone's food without paying for it. Instead, we worked night and day with effort and hard work so that we would not impose on you. We did this to give you an example to imitate, not because we didn't have a right to insist on financial support. Even when we were with you we were giving you this command: "If anyone doesn't want to work, they shouldn't eat." We hear that some of you are living an undisciplined life. They aren't working, but they are meddling in other people's business. By the Lord Jesus Christ, we command and encourage such people to work quietly and put their own food on the table. Brothers and sisters, don't get discouraged in doing what is right.

2 Thessalonians 3:6-13

Prayer

God, may I use my spare time in a way that pleases you. Help me to develop the consistent practices needed to use the time I have wisely. Keep me from procrastinating in order that I might find more free time to honor and glorify you. Amen.

We tend to think that only the egomaniac is self-centered. In fact, we all possess the narcissistic inclination to think of and act for ourselves first.

Chapter 14

AM I SELF-CONSCIOUS, SELF-PITYING, OR SELF-JUSTIFYING?

It is healthy to be self-aware. To know ourselves well helps us to navigate decisions, avoid giving into temptations, cautiously respond to someone we disagree with, know the areas in which we need help or support, and, generally speaking, helps us to live a holistic life of Christian formation.

However, being too aware of self can make us self-absorbed if we're not careful. We all get like this from time to time. You can see it when we are quickly defensive, when an attitude of preeminence creeps in, when insecurities rise, when compassion and understanding are hard to notice within, when being right becomes more important than being generous, when we hide our true self in fear of being found out or realized, and when we are quick to blame others for our own shortcomings. Wesley wants us to reflect and discuss the question, "Am I self-conscious, self-pitying, or self-justifying?" so that we confront our human penchant to be so concerned with self that we lose sight of the others in our lives.

Genesis 3 is the first place in Scripture where we see how a propensity for being concerned with self can cause one to lose a sense of all reality. It can make us forget our purpose for living, which is to bring glory to God. In Genesis 3, we learn that Adam and Eve find the fruit of the Tree of the Knowledge of Good and Evil to be good for food and pleasing to the eye. God has asked Adam and Eve to steer clear of the tree, as eating from it would bring them face to face with sin.

Although Adam and Eve had this instruction from God, the message of the serpent and the temptation of the fruit were too much to bear. As a result, Adam and Eve usurped God's authority by eating the fruit and subsequently found themselves in the grip of two emotions they had never felt before. Before eating the fruit, Adam and Eve weren't aware of feelings such as guilt and shame, which cause anxiety—the kind of anxiety that makes you cover up and hide. Ultimately, these new feelings of guilt and shame lead to Adam being so self-absorbed that when God comes looking for them and asks Adam why they are hiding, Adam declares that he is afraid because he has done what God has asked him not to do. Adam's moment of blame shifting, if you will, comes when he tells God, "The woman you gave me, she gave me some fruit from the tree, and I ate." Eve's response is similar. She says, "The snake tricked me, and I ate." Both Adam and Eve (because of their guilt and shame) place the blame on others.

This human desire to blame others comes from self-absorption. We become so ensnared in our own feelings, whatever they may be, and whatever they may result from, that we deliberately protect our own status, wanting others to believe that we are not at fault. This is one of the common struggles of humanity across all time. The story of Adam and Eve is an archetypal story—it represents or symbolizes an original incident that continues to be imitated. As quickly as we blame Adam and Eve for the brokenness of our world, we take any sense of responsibility and shift it on to someone else.

Defeatist and defensive behaviors and insecurities will exist in us and in others. This is one of the main points of the Adam and Eve story. No one is exempt from these feelings and behaviors rising up on occasion. Discussing them with our loved ones is the best way to acknowledge, admit, and take action to rid these from our daily life. We tend to think that only the egomaniac is self-centered. In fact, we all possess the narcissistic inclination to think of and act for ourselves first.

So, then, how can we combat these feelings of guilt and shame that eventually direct us toward self-centeredness? Here are seven simple ways to meet the temptation for self-absorption head-on:

Today's Challenge

Do something outside of your comfort zone today. Talk to a stranger, invite someone you don't know well out to lunch, take treats to the neighbors who keep to themselves— whatever it is, it needs to be something that makes you a little nervous and uncomfortable before you take it on.

1. **Volunteer/Serve:** It is amazing how serving someone else or championing a social cause can change you from being *about you* to being more the *real you*. Feed homeless people, help repair a house, participate in disaster relief, rescue a pet—serve others.

2. **Engage in random acts of kindness:** You don't have to formally commit to volunteer work or social causes that appear to others to be a big deal. Sometimes the best way to become less self-centered is to go out of your way to brighten someone else's day—flowers, thank-you cards, smiles, conversations, and the like can go a long way. Hint: don't engage in kindness to impress others; then you are right back where you started.

3. **Practice empathy:** When was the last time you really listened to another person's story? Empathy can be practiced in all kinds of ways, but one of the best disciplines is to genuinely listen to someone who is hurting or, on the flip side, celebrating. Joining people

in their mourning or in their rejoicing takes the focus off of self.

4. **Compete—knowing you will lose:** What are you not good at? Find something you are not good at, compete hard, but just know you are going to lose. Perhaps a game of tennis or golf? Maybe you could play a video game with your kid and get creamed. What if you joined in on the neighborhood card game knowing you hate cards and will lose? Losing, appropriately, can put things into perspective really quickly.

5. **Get out of your comfort zone:** Do something you hate doing or that takes you out of your comfort zone. Talk to a stranger or volunteer to give that presentation you are so afraid to give. Write a letter of thanks to your boss even if others may misconstrue it as sucking up. When you make yourself do something that is a complete stretch, that others might do better than you, it can help keep you grounded, humble, and knowing you need support.

6. **Let someone else lead for once:** Calling all control freaks! Give up the map, steering wheel, or the helm and let someone else navigate the way for a change. Choosing to follow others is a great way to become less self-centered.

7. **Begin to know someone you find hard to like:** We all know personalities clash. Find a person you know you will find hard to like and spend some time with them. Caution: Don't let them become an agenda. Instead, truly try to overcome your dislike by developing a genuine interest in them. Spending time with people whom we find hard to like will help us from becoming self-centered. (By the way, there is someone who doesn't like you too. It doesn't just go one way.)

Do yourself a favor. Reflect carefully and act swiftly on the core of what Wesley was getting at in the question, "Am I self-conscious, self-pitying, or self-justifying?" and watch it change the way you see the world and also the way others see you.

Reflection Questions

1. Has anyone ever accused you of being self-absorbed, self-pitying, or self-justifying? Most of us have probably heard that at least once in our lives. What were the circumstances of that encounter? Did you learn anything about yourself as a result?

2. How often do you attempt something you will be "bad" at? If your answer is "rarely," why do you think that is? Are you afraid of being embarrassed or looking foolish to others? Are you worried about criticism, or is it because you like to be best?

Personal Application Ideas

1. Engage in random acts of kindness this week. Buy the coffee of the person behind you in line. Offer compliments and smiles as you go about your day.

2. Do something outside of your comfort zone, or something that you are "bad" at. Does your partner love to dance, but you hate it? Go dancing anyway. In public. With enthusiasm. Fight against your urge to feel self-conscious or self-absorbed.

---

scripture

Don't do anything for selfish purposes, but with humility think of others as better than yourselves. Instead of each person watching out for their own good, watch out for what is better for others.

Philippians 2:3-4

Prayer

God, teach me to serve you first and to seek your Kingdom. Help me to be less concerned about myself and more about you and your mission for this world. Help me to be aware of myself, my faults, and limitations, but also not to be so concerned with myself that I forget your purpose for me. Amen.

Section 3

RELATIONSHIP WITH OTHERS: AN OUTWARD FOCUS

Section 3

RELATIONSHIP WITH OTHERS: AN OUTWARD FOCUS

Authentic followers of Jesus know that to neglect or mistreat others is to neglect and mistreat Jesus. Throughout the Gospels, Jesus teaches us that the way we treat others is a direct reflection on our love for him. Deeply committed Christians—those who live with a total love for God and others—must pay careful attention to how we think about and interact with others.

Wesley's questions challenge us to think beyond self and toward how we treat others to help us on our way to a life in the way of Jesus. His pointed questions can expose how we truly feel about our fellow human beings. In asking the questions, Wesley intended to push Christians past superficiality in our relationships with others and toward a penetrating depth marked by generosity and compassion.

God established four spheres of relationship when creating the world. God founded the relationship between God and humans, humans and the cosmos, humans and self, and humans and other humans. A deep level of intimacy in every sense marked each of the four spheres of relationships God instituted. God clearly desired that humans would enjoy life inside the cosmos together. How we live life with others is clearly important to God's plan for our world.

As you continue reflecting on your life through Wesley's questions, it is important not only to view your relationships with others on a personal level but also on a missional level. God's mission is to restore the world toward its intended wholeness. This means that Christians are challenged as agents or ambassadors of God's love to participate with God to restore the world.

Sometimes the most impactful ways we can participate in God's mission is to make sure that the relationships in our homes, churches, workplaces, and communities are characterized by wholeness or peace. As Christians accepting the challenge to love God and love others, we must work toward creating relationships that honor God. The way we treat our spouse or partners, our children, our employees, and our neighbors matters.

If God's mission is to restore the world to its intended wholeness and we are God's chosen vehicles to represent God's mission, then we must make our concern for others a top priority. As you read, reflect, and pray in the coming days, be sure to remember that the biggest impact we can make in the whole world around us is often to the people right in front of us.

Chapter 15

DO I THANK GOD THAT I AM NOT LIKE OTHERS?

Jesus is a master storyteller. The stories Jesus tells are meant to help us think, feel, and be. They are meant, ultimately, to shape us or transform us toward the likeness of Christ—to live like Christ. Although not always easy to interpret at first, Jesus' brilliantly piercing stories are designed to move us away from where we are in our weakness toward new or renewed strength in our pursuit of a Christlike life.

In Luke 18, Jesus tells a story of two men who go to the temple to pray. One man, a Pharisee (a Jewish leader), prays, and as he prays he compares himself to another person who happens to be praying near him. He brags about his religious accomplishments and at the same time points to a man near him and tells God of his thankfulness in not being like this man. By contrast, the man the Pharisee is speaking about is a tax collector, and when he approaches God, he can only find the strength to cry out, "God, show mercy to me, a sinner."

There are many insights to be drawn from Jesus' story. Chief among them is this: We are not to compare ourselves to others. We are to evaluate our own spiritual maturity based on what God desires from us, not from what we may find as failings and faults in another person's life. To thank God that we are not like others, as the Pharisee in Jesus' story did, is to arrogantly and shortsightedly see ourselves in a false light. God doesn't desire our being better than another. Rather, God desires that we become the best possible individuals we've been created to be.

Humans are good at comparing. We have a tendency to find our self-worth in the midst of another person's situation, particularly, if we are honest, in their misfortune. We compare ourselves on the wealth we have accumulated. We compare ourselves to others on the personal possessions we have. We compare ourselves on our children's schools, the neighborhoods we live in, and our places of employment. Comparing ourselves to others, for whatever reason, is a dangerous exercise that creates a false reality.

Sometimes we compare ourselves to others to find reasons that we are better. On the other hand, sometimes we compare ourselves to others in our "woe is me" mind-set, believing that because we do not have a high-paying job or a big house or a perfect family like the others we see around us, we are not as good as they are. This exercise is just as dangerous as comparing ourselves to others to prove how good we are. The situations we find ourselves in, such as poverty, joblessness, illness, or addiction, may or may not be a direct result of decisions we have made. Regardless of what we face, we are not unworthy people. All of creation is God's and God's love reaches to include every one of us. We are all worthy in God's eyes.

A few months ago I was headed to a football game with a friend. As we sat in the car in line to pay for parking, my friend turned to me and said, "It's not fair that I have to drive this piece of junk when he gets to drive that!" He pointed out the window at a bright red Porsche. My friend went on, "People think I am a nothing in this old car. If I had a car like that, I'd be set." Not exactly the same scenario as the story Jesus tells in Luke 18, but still an illustration of thinking that somehow what we have or who we are in others' eyes is more significant than being real at the feet of God.

Comparing our situation to others' is not healthy. Whether thanking God for not being like others or wishing God would give us what others have, we are discrediting God. Your worth is not found in how much more religious you think you are than others, or how much more religious you wish you were in order to be like others.

To get back to the crux of Wesley's question, we must realize that we all have issues in life that keep us from the true identity God has designed for us. This realization should bring us before God in a similar spirit as the tax collector in Jesus' story in Luke 18. When we come before God acknowledging our place before him (God is God and we are not), our posture leads us toward deeper humility, which ultimately takes from us feelings of judgment and comparison to become people of grace, mercy, and care. Let's choose to think the best of people and see others through a lens of hope, not a lens of disgust.

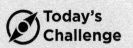

Today's Challenge

Count the number of times you compare yourself to others today. You'll have to develop a heightened awareness, but you may find the number shocking! Think about every news story you read or watch, every Facebook post you glance at, every meeting you attend, every person you look at in the gym. What are the comparisons you make?

Reflection Questions

1. How do you compare yourself to others? Do you tend to find yourself lacking in some way, or do you find you are grateful that you are not like them?
2. Who do you most often compare yourself to? Is there one particular person or group of people that draw this tendency out in you? Why is that the case?

Personal Application Ideas

1. Identify the triggers for the times you compare yourself to others. Perhaps the Facebook posts of your acquaintances

leave you feeling either defeated, or somewhat self-satisfied. Perhaps a club you're involved in causes you to feel less than others in some way. Remove these triggers from your life for a period of time. What is the result?

2. The next time you find yourself thanking God that you are not like a particular person or that you are not in a particular situation, dig deeply. How pure are your feelings of thankfulness?

---

scripture

Therefore, as God's choice, holy and loved, put on compassion, kindness, humility, gentleness, and patience.

Colossians 3:12

Prayer

Oh, God, help me to be humble in my actions, words, and thoughts. Teach me to see others as you see them—through a lens of love, compassion, and mercy. I pray that I might always remember that we are all lost without you. Amen.

Chapter 16

AM I CONSCIOUSLY OR UNCONSCIOUSLY CREATING THE IMPRESSION THAT I AM BETTER THAN I AM? IN OTHER WORDS, AM I A HYPOCRITE?

Contributed by Chris Abel

There is a saying that perhaps you've heard: "Fake it 'til you make it." But when does faking it actually make anything? If you fake your medical license, you will go to jail. If you fake that wedding ring, the only thing you'll "make" is a hurt spouse. You can't make a cake with fake flour. It's a weird saying, right?

And yet, we encourage people to fake it when it comes to life. Whoever first invented this saying probably did so to encourage us when we struggle with self-doubt. And to some extent there is a truth here. Each of us has roles we play that make us question if we're enough. Will I be a good leader? parent? child? artist? athlete? spouse? Will people respect me? Will they like me?

What the phrase really means to say is this: "Don't entertain your doubt. Eventually you will feel some confidence." But many of us get stuck. We live a half-finished idiom: "Fake it."

How many of us never feel competent, never feel loved or accepted, and easily feel threatened? We make our cake with fake flour, and we're afraid someone might take a bite and see through the icing.

This is a hard question to ask yourself, but Wesley prompted it for a very good reason. See, when you fake it, you don't actually make it. Faking it—pretending to be better than we are—actually keeps us from knowing who we are and how we are doing. When we put up a facade, we freeze our growth.

Growth cannot come from faking it.

Elon Musk, founder of PayPal, Tesla, and SpaceX, understands this concept, even in a business environment. In an interview, he once said, "I think it's very important to have a feedback loop, where you're constantly thinking about what you've done and how you could be doing it better. I think that's the single best piece of advice: constantly think about how you could be doing things better and questioning yourself."[1]

When you're honest with yourself, you open the door to growth. When you're honest with yourself, you begin to tap into the potential that God has in store for you. When you're honest with yourself, you stop faking it and start moving toward something greater. This is why grace is so powerful. It means that God isn't interested in blame or shame. God forgives because God wants you to be the fullest, most alive version of yourself.

Wesley believed that God could so greatly move in someone's life that they could reach harmony with God *in this life*. He believed that we have incredible potential and are not slaves to our flaws and selfish inclinations. He called it "sanctification." It will take time and work. But God wants you to face yourself as you truly are because it is the doorway to seeing *who you can become*.

You have incredible potential. This is why you don't need to fake it. This is why you don't need to create an impression that you are better than you are. You, as you are, with all your cracks and flaws and blemishes, are amazing.

In the Book of Philippians, the author makes an interesting point about Jesus: "Though he was in the form of God, / he did not consider being equal with God something to exploit. / But he emptied himself / by taking the form of a slave / and by becoming like human beings" (Philippians 2:6-7).

His point? No faking it here. Jesus was well aware of his status and abilities. He was in tune with his life and place in the whole of reality. And his place was very, very high. He wasn't concerned with appearances. There are even moments in the hours leading up to his death where he could have *talked his way out of crucifixion*. He could have cleared his name or defended himself. Instead, Jesus remained silent, unconcerned with the impressions of his interrogators. He didn't need to prove anything to anyone.

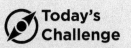

Today's Challenge

Ask someone you trust to name an area of your life in which you appear to be faking it. Encourage them to be honest with you. How can you move from a place of falsehood and putting on a brave face to a place of authenticity and growth?

So often in life, we struggle with appearances. We can't bear to have our name slandered. We need to be liked. We dress to create a persona that more people will find attractive. We create piles of wealth, hoping that perhaps our finances might make us important. We strive to be seen as smart/creative/athletic/artistic. The list goes on.

The danger here is that we create a fake life. We try to prove something by faking it until we finally build the facades so high we can't climb out of the caricatures we've created. That's not living. By faking it, we fail to receive the very thing we are looking for: respect and approval. Even if we achieve it, people admire the false version of ourselves. What happens when you retire? when you age? when you make a mistake? Then suddenly the approval is gone. That kind of attention isn't loyal. It's never satisfying. It's fickle, and it will leave you in a heartbeat.

God doesn't want the fake version of you. God wants the real you, the authentic, flawed, real version of you. God doesn't need you to be perfect or to know exactly who you are and where you're going. God isn't interested in judging or blaming. God is interested in growth. In love. In honesty.

And when you find this version of yourself, you will be free. You will be free from living a life of constantly seeking approval. You will be able to handle criticism. You will be able to own your mistakes. You will be able to grow.

Reflection Questions

1. Who do I have in my life who knows the real me?
2. How can I be more real with people?
3. Do I have environments where I feel like I have to fake it? Why?

Personal Application Ideas

1. Write a letter to yourself with three areas of your life you would like to see grow. Seal it and save it. (Or e-mail at futureme.org)
2. Develop a mentor relationship with someone who can provide you honest feedback.
3. If you have a family, come up with a family growth plan for the year.

---

scripture

God didn't give us a spirit that is timid but one that is powerful, loving, and self-controlled.

2 Timothy 1:7

Prayer

God, help us to see ourselves as we truly are. Keep us from creating false versions of ourselves, and let us be surrounded by people who we can be real with. Empower us with energy and attitude to continue growing and seeking your will in our lives. Amen.

When we as Christians cannot keep secrets or hold confidential matters private, we sabotage the very sense of community Jesus came to create.

Chapter 17

DO I CONFIDENTIALLY PASS ON TO OTHERS WHAT WAS TOLD TO ME IN CONFIDENCE?

Keeping confidential matters confidential builds trust, and we all know that one of the fundamental essentials of establishing and sustaining strong relationships is trust. Trust is the complete confidence that you can rely on another to responsibly and faithfully keep your best interests in mind. Trust is the key to any and all healthy relationships.

But trust is hard to come by. I have shared personal and intimate matters of my life with others in what I thought was complete confidence, only to have it come back to me that my confidential matter became public. You've probably had this happen too. When this happens, it can destroy the relationship because trust is the foundation on which relationships start and remain strong.

Why do we feel the need to share matters told to us in confidence? It is simple, really. We feel the need to relay private information because information is power. Humans love power, and we love to let others know that we have access to powerful information. What we fail to realize, however, is that once the information is shared, it is no longer filled with power. The power of private information shared outside the bounds of trust turns us into people enslaved by the very power we wish to demonstrate. When we break confidence, we are subjected to the power of suspicion, doubt, and skepticism.

When we as Christians cannot keep secrets or hold confidential matters private, we sabotage the very sense of community Jesus came to create. Jesus modeled for all of us what it looks like to give your life away to someone with a complete sense of trust and dependence. Not holding private matters confidential drives a wedge between people, prevents growth in relationships, and, therefore, can create doubt and insecurity. Any relationship is doomed if doubt and insecurity are its foundational elements. When friends, coworkers, spouses, partners, siblings, and children no longer feel safe, you have created a devastating environment that even the most sincere apology can never ultimately repair.

A few months ago, I met a friend for lunch—let's call him Roger. Roger wanted to talk to me about how to rebuild his relationship with his business partner, Mary (also not her real name). Roger and Mary were lifelong friends, having grown up together in a small, rural town. Their farms literally were divided by a barbed-wired fence. They saw each other every day for years.

After hearing about how Roger abused his position as Mary's friend by revealing to some clients and employees personal information Mary shared with him, I wasn't sure the two would remain business partners or ever be friends again. The last time I saw Roger, he said Mary hasn't spoken to him in months and they sold the business. Their families once shared a meal together at least once a week but hadn't been together in months. Breaking trust by revealing information we are asked to keep confidential can destroy friends and family.

Yes, there are times when confidential matters should be made public. If the information you learn from another is either harming the person sharing the information or is harming another, it should be revealed appropriately. I was once asked to keep a secret that I did not keep. Someone told me he was an alcoholic and that his disease had gotten so out of control that he was driving while intoxicated nearly every time he got in a car. This is not something to keep confidential. There is an appropriate way to handle the information, but it mustn't be kept silent.

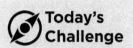

Today's Challenge

Think of the most trustworthy friend you have, and take time today to thank this person for the trust established in your relationship. Tell this person of the value you place on such a presence in your life.

When we break trust by sharing information told to us in confidence, we damage our character. When we damage our character we work against God's design for a good world. We work to become holy people with character that is described by others as integrity, trustworthiness, and reliability so that we can reveal a snapshot of who Jesus Christ is to the world around us. We are to live like Christ, and to live like Christ is to be a person with character.

We all have friends who come to us with others' personal information. Perhaps we are the ones known to our friends as this kind of friend. The next time a friend, coworker, employee, or sibling comes to you with another's confidential information, how will you handle it? How will you work to be as Christ is?

Reflection Questions

1. Have you ever betrayed someone's confidence? What were the circumstances?
2. If you have ever betrayed someone's confidence, how did you feel after you shared that person's confidential information? Are you still in a relationship with that person? Why or why not?
3. If you have never betrayed someone's confidence, how was this principle of trust instilled in you?

Personal Application Ideas

1. The next time you are tempted to divulge someone's confidential information in any way, stop yourself and say this prayer to yourself—or out loud: "Jesus Christ, Son of

the living God, have mercy on me, a sinner." Repeat the prayer until you are no longer tempted to act in a way that Christ would not act.

2. If you have betrayed someone's trust in the past but have not apologized or been reconciled, pray and ask God for guidance and courage in this situation. Consider reaching out and apologizing for the harm you may have caused.

scripture

A slanderer walks around revealing secrets,
  but a trustworthy person keeps a confidence.

Proverbs 11:13

Prayer

Help me, God, to control my desire to reveal information that was told to me in confidence. Help me also to guard my tongue and to think before I speak and act. Amen.

Chapter 18

AM I JEALOUS, IMPURE, CRITICAL, IRRITABLE, TOUCHY, OR DISTRUSTFUL?

If I am honest, my answer to all of the above is a disheartening, "Yes." I don't like that I possess these types of behavior, but I do. I am working on becoming less of all of the above. Maybe one day I will be able to remove them from my way of life altogether, but, for now, I am pursuing a long winding path toward being less jealous, less impure, and less critical.

What is it that makes me want what others have? What is it about myself that allows my tainted feelings toward someone to ruin my day, and in some cases, another's day as well? Why do I feel the need to criticize things that are not even my responsibility, and in some cases don't even affect me personally? Why do I make needless remarks to my wife and kids, proving my irritability? Most often, it is because I allow my circumstances and situations to direct my behavior.

These behaviors live inside all of us. When we express them, however, they become an issue that must be addressed. God's desire is for us to be strong people, meaning we are to be resilient enough and disciplined enough to keep our emotions in check. God desires that we keep the above characteristics, and ones like them, from adversely impacting our life and the lives of others around us.

Emotional tendencies like jealousy, irritability, and distrust are poisons that can spread to impact every area of our life if we are not careful. When this happens, it can cripple us. For some, it is like a downward spiral or vicious cycle. We let an unfortunate incident make us short-tempered. We express our frustration by snapping at someone or getting snarky. Our snarky behavior is passed on to others who are now also frustrated with us. This kind of uncontrolled emotional release creates unnecessary tension or strain on our relationships, and it can be hard to work our way out of the mess we've created and unfortunately brought others into.

A few years ago in a discussion with my wife I blurted out the general statement that "you can't trust anyone!" I said this in anger as I was recounting a series of events that led to a disagreement with several of my colleagues. My wife, in her immeasurable wisdom, said, "You don't really mean that, do you?" I shook my head in silence, still fuming from what had happened earlier in the day. "If you really think that you can't trust anyone, that is a very sad place to be. I think that says more about you than it does your colleagues."

My wife was right. If I can't live trusting others, then what do I have? All I have is trust in myself, which merely creates separation and ultimately isolation. To be cautious or even suspicious is one thing. To live distrustfully, as Wesley names it in the question above, is to have zero confidence in anyone. If we don't have confidence in others, we can't think the best of others. If we can't think the best of others, we can't trust others. If we can't trust others, we can never truly find the community that we long for.

Whether you are dealing with jealousy, irritability, or a critical spirit, there are several ways to develop the discipline and strength to keep our emotions and emotionally charged behaviors in check.

First, develop the discipline to **delay your reaction**. Have you ever said something in haste only to have it be false or embarrassing? Have you ever jumped to conclusions and reacted emotionally, only to find out there was no need for the outburst? Instead of doing or saying something you'll regret, take a deep breath, count to ten, assess the situation, and try and remain calm, distancing your emotional response from the incident or situation.

Second, **find a healthy outlet** for your frustrations and irritations. Is there someone you can confide in? Is there a series of memorized verses you can quote? Is there a prayer you can whisper? Is there a song you can sing? Find what works for you, but find something that quiets the soul in a way that keeps you from erupting.

Third, work to **see the irritation, frustration, or other feeling in the context of the greater whole of your life**. Far too often, we lash out or react quickly in a variety of ways that shrink our whole life into the moment we find ourselves in. We can inadvertently get blurry or tunnel vision and, due to our reaction, only see what is a foot in front of us instead of seeing what has just occurred in the context of the greater whole.

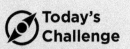

Today's Challenge

Force yourself to pause when an event or conversation triggers an emotional response in you. Tempted to confront someone driving poorly when you are out in traffic? Hit the pause button. Feel like responding sarcastically to a comment from your spouse or coworker? Take a deep breath and delay.

Finally, **ask God to give you peace**. Ask for divine help in the moment of high emotion and keep in mind that everything that happens to us in life helps us to become more like Christ. I realize this is easier said than done, but what isn't? The famous preacher A. W. Tozer once said, "When I understand that everything happening to me is to make me more Christ-like, it resolves a great deal of anxiety in our lives."[1] God can grant you the serenity you need to handle the stressors that come your way.

Reflection Questions

1. Which of the characteristics John Wesley calls out in this question do you most struggle with?
2. Do you have a close relationship with someone who displays these behaviors on a regular basis? What is the impact on you?

Personal Application Ideas

1. The next time you find yourself reacting irritably to someone or feeling jealousy toward another person, take a moment to ask yourself what is really driving your emotions. You may have to wait until the "smoke clears," and you feel calm again. But take the time to question yourself and understand what is triggering your negative responses.

2. Identity some healthy outlets for your frustrations and tensions—exercise (even a quick walk around the block), breath prayers, meditation, a gratitude journal, playing with your dogs—there are many possibilities.

---

scripture

My dear friends, since we have these promises, let's cleanse ourselves from anything that contaminates our body or spirit so that we make our holiness complete in the fear of God.

2 Corinthians 7:1

Prayer

Holy Spirit, breathe in me so that my thoughts may be pure.
Holy Spirit, move in me so that my work may be pure.
Holy Spirit, pull me into your love so that I love only what is pure.
Holy Spirit, give me the strength to guard my heart so that all I do is pure.
Amen.

Chapter 19

AM I HONEST IN ALL MY ACTIONS AND WORDS, OR DO I EXAGGERATE?

My family moved around a lot when I was a child and teenager. Before my dad became a pastor, he served for ten years or so in the US Navy. Much of my childhood is a blur to me. We moved often enough that I felt like I was always scrambling to make new friends. Part of my *modus operandi* was to make up stories about my past. I would often exaggerate the stories that were real in order to present myself in a better light. It was simple. I wanted people to like me so I would make up stories or exaggerate in order to make people think I was interesting enough to be friends with.

I vividly remember telling my friends that my older brother had a fiery red Corvette, and that when I was older he was going to give it to me to drive. When my friends met my brother for the first time, they watched him climb out of a rusty old pickup truck. One of my friends asked, "Where is your Corvette?" "Corvette!" my brother replied. "Ha! I wish. Chris, have you been telling stories again?" he asked. I was embarrassed, and my true self was revealed. I was a storyteller, or as my grandfather would call me on occasion, a "fibber."

Wesley meant this question to do three things, I think. First, his question is meant to help us evaluate our level of contentment with life. Are we content, or do we live in a mode of constant aspiration?

To be content is to accept what we have in life, to be grateful for it and, therefore, to be satisfied and able to find joy. Contentment comes from a spirit of gratitude. God desires that we are grateful people who learn to make the most of what we have.

Second, this question is meant to help us be true to our identity in Christ, not to our identity in self. When we find our identity in Christ, we recognize that we are valued as a person regardless of our success or failure, our possessions or poverty, or our significance or silent obscurity. Christ loves us for who we are as a child of God, not for what we do or have.

Finally, I believe Wesley wants us to reflect on our character. We are, after all, made in the image of God. We've been created to reflect the love of God to everyone we come into contact with. We cannot appropriately reflect or radiate this holy love of God to all if we are not living into the image in which we've been created. As Christians, when we lie, deceive, or even unintentionally exaggerate, we present God in a way that is not worthy of God's honor and glory. To find a deep sense of union with God, self, and others, we must be people who are honest and trustworthy. Remember, we are the physical representation of Jesus on this earth. We are the hands, feet, eyes, ears, and body of Jesus.

"I'm stuck, Chris," a friend confided in me. "What do you mean by stuck?" I replied. This friend went on, "I have been lying to my friends. I told them my parents have a lake house and that is where I go on the weekends when I am not around. I don't have a lake house. I go visit my brother, who is in prison. I don't want my friends to know that my brother is in prison—so I made up the lake house story. Now they want to know if they can come hang out at the lake house with me. That is what I mean by I am stuck."

For a host of reasons, my heart sank for this friend as we charted a course for telling his friends the truth and asking them to forgive him. To his credit, he had the guts to carry out our plan—he came clean. I asked him several weeks later, "How are you doing? How do you feel?" He answered, "I feel free, like I don't have anything to hide anymore. Oh, and actually, my friends are driving me up to see my brother next weekend."

Sometimes we lie. Sometimes we exaggerate. Sometimes we pretend we are more important than we really are. We want to be liked so we add on or take away from the truth so that we are seen in a more positive light. We all know that if people do not accept us for who we really are, then they are not really our true friends. It is hard, however, because we compare ourselves to those we want to be like. We want to be admired for our greatness, when the true call of the Christian life is to decrease in order that Christ might increase (see John 3:30).

> ## Today's Challenge
>
> Commit to a "no exaggeration, no lie" policy for the next twenty-four hours. Resist the urge to blame a traffic jam on your lateness or to extend the size of that fish you caught as you tell the story.

Be encouraged, however! God is a God of second chances. Throughout the Bible, we have numerous stories of people who have deceived God or others (think of Jacob's deceit) and whom God has forgiven and welcomed with open arms.

Friend, don't waste your time running around trying to keep your lie or exaggeration afloat. Instead, confess your offense and live in freedom from the guilt, shame, and indignity. Your reputation may take a hit. Your friends or family may be cynically surprised, but your honesty just might win them over.

Be content. Be grateful. Be you. Live inspired by your heavenly worth! When you get to heaven and stand before God, God will not ask you, "Why weren't you more like the Apostle Paul or Peter?" Instead God will ask you, "How come you weren't the you I created you to be?"

Reflection Questions

1. Do you find yourself exaggerating when you recount a story to another person? If so, what is driving that urge? Are you worried that your reality is not interesting enough to someone else?
2. Have you ever been caught in a lie? What was the situation? What did you learn from it?

Personal Application Ideas

1. Is there a truth you need to tell someone? Do you need to "come clean" about something? Set aside some private time with that person and confess your truth.
2. Notice the circumstances the next time you are tempted to lie or exaggerate. What is driving this temptation? Are you intimidated by the group you are with? Do you feel "less than" in some way? Are you trying to impress someone?

---

scripture

Don't lie to each other. Take off the old human nature with its practices and put on the new nature, which is renewed in knowledge by conforming to the image of the one who created it. In this image there is neither Greek nor Jew, circumcised nor uncircumcised, barbarian, Scythian, slave nor free, but Christ is all things and in all people.

Colossians 3:9-11

Prayer

Jesus, you have modeled honesty—from your birth to your death, burial, and resurrection. I pray that honesty may become one of my most valued and tangible virtues. Direct my thoughts, words, and actions that I may enhance all of the relationships I am in—at home, work, school, and places of recreation. Amen.

Chapter 20

IS THERE ANYONE WHOM
I FEAR, DISLIKE, DISOWN, CRITICIZE,
HOLD RESENTMENT TOWARD,
OR DISREGARD?

We cannot fully live the Christian life, as Jesus meant us to, until we are at peace not only with God and ourselves but also with others. To be wholly Christian, therefore, means to be like Christ. Christ modeled for us a life of wholly surrendering to God and called us to live a life like that, a life in which we have a complete and total love for God and others. This is what it means to be a deeply committed Christian.

Today's question covers a lot of ground. Taking into account the people we fear, those we feel disdain or indifference toward, and the people we resent can amount to a few people or many. The answer will look different in each of our lives. We likely fear some people, disdain others, and resent still others. Each of our lives can encompass a range of these feelings.

This relational separation is not what Jesus wants for our lives. Jesus demonstrates a love for *all* people in *all* situations. Even when Jesus criticizes his disciples for one thing or another, he still loves with a love so fierce and relentless that the disciples know that love underlies his corrective words. Jesus teaches us that to look upon another in any way other than love, for whatever reason, is short-circuiting the Christian life.

We typically feel fear, dislike, or resentment toward others because of several factors. First, we assume we are better than they are. We are a better leader, a better athlete, a better parent, or a better spouse. Comparing ourselves to others is dangerous. Comparing ourselves with others creates a mentality of separation. We create distance from others in our lives and, therefore, build walls of dislike, criticism, and sometimes even bitterness. Rather than looking through a lens of comparison, Christians must look through a lens of compassion. We must work to see people as God sees them—as beloved children of great value and worth.

I have a friend who often completely embarrasses me. He is loud and often obnoxious. He's the guy we've all seen in the restaurant who is so loud that every head in the room turns his way, frequently in complete and utter disgust. Once, in fact, he was so loud—just laughing and having a good time—that the manager came to our table and told us we'd had too much to drink, and if we didn't quiet down he would ask us to leave. We weren't even drinking! My friend is so loud and gets so carried away that he can't seem to control his behavior. This makes for very embarrassing situations. So what are my options? Do I pretend he is not my friend and dismiss him? Do I simply let him be who he is and love him anyway? Do I love him so much that I tell him the truth about how others perceive him? I believe the latter is best—I love him so much that I must tell him why it is that others choose not to be around him. He's a likable guy and very shy at first, but watch out. There is a tendency for me to compare my behavior to his, and in so doing, start to see myself as more socially aware or, if I am truly honest, better than he is, because I would never act like he does. This is what comparing ourselves to others can do—create separation.

Second, we develop distance from others in our lives because we don't like their personality. We use phrases like "rubs me the wrong way" or "we're on different pages" or "drives me crazy." These, and other phrases like them, tend to create distance from the very people we are called to love. Imagine if Jesus had said, "I wish I had never called Simon Peter along on this journey with the rest of us. He just rubs me the wrong way. He doesn't think before he acts—he just needs to use his head."

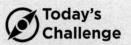

Today's Challenge

Take a minute to talk with a person whom you fear, dislike, criticize, or disregard. Show this person the love of Christ.

It is true: You will never be fully compatible with everyone else around you. Some people's persona or disposition will drive you crazy. However, who are we called to be? Are we called to be people who are compatible or people who are compassionate? Compassion for the other, as Jesus showed time and time again, will move us past the limitations of compatibility and toward unlimited, generous concern and compassion for others.

Several years ago I was leading a team on a project to help people in their faith development and formation. I had people from all backgrounds on my team. One day one of the members of the team came to me and said, "I can't do this anymore. ['So and so'] is driving me crazy!" About an hour later 'So and So' came to me and said, "I can't function well on this team. ['What's his name'] is totally unbearable and very annoying." I kid you not—the two were talking about each other! Sometimes the distance we create and keep between ourselves and other people can create a false sense of whose persona is actually superior. For every person who "drives you crazy" there is a person whom you "drive crazy" too.

A third reason we tend to push people away and resent them is due to the belief that the other has somehow wronged us. Typically, when someone wrongs us, our inability to forgive keeps us from wanting to even be around that person or those people. I've seen this in my family firsthand, and I would venture to say that you probably have too. Sometimes the feelings of resentment stem from a very real and painful situation or set of circumstances that give us a strong desire to neglect (or even hide from) the people who've hurt us. This is a natural human defense mechanism. It is not, however, a healthy way to live. We must confess our resentment and work hard at forgiving the people who have wronged us. This is not easy or simple. It can often take years to mend or heal broken relationships.

Jesus wants us to be reconciled. Jesus wants us to experience the peace of God in all areas of our life. We are called to regard all with love. Regardless of how hard it may be, a challenge in the Christian life is to be like Christ—loving toward all.

Reflection Questions

1. Would you say you are at peace with God, self, and others? Why or why not?
2. Have you created or kept separation between you and another because you simply don't like them? If so, ask yourself what is driving this dislike.
3. Is there a very good reason why you hold resentment toward another person? In what way can you reconcile this?

Personal Application Ideas

1. Find a moment today to say a kind thing to a person you dislike or have intentionally steered clear of.
2. Sometime this week, if the occasion presents itself or if you can make it present itself, speak with a person who "rubs you the wrong way."
3. Pray that God would grant you the courage and grace to find a way to forgive a person who has wronged you in some way.

scripture

Love is patient, love is kind, it isn't jealous, it doesn't brag, it isn't arrogant, it isn't rude, it doesn't seek its own advantage, it isn't irritable, it doesn't keep a record of complaints, it isn't happy with injustice, but it is happy with the truth. Love puts up with all things, trusts in all things, hopes for all things, endures all things.

Love never fails. As for prophecies, they will be brought to an end. As for tongues, they will stop. As for knowledge, it will be brought to an end.

1 Corinthians 13:4-8

Prayer

Lord, change us. Remove the tendency for us to compare ourselves with others and think we are better than they are. Replace comparison with compassion and make us more like Christ is—loving to all. Jesus, we pray that we may be reconciled to all those toward whom we hold resentment or dislike. Amen.

To respond faithfully to Wesley's question, "When did I last speak about my faith?" is to live a life of going, obeying, and listening to the Holy Spirit, realizing that each one of us is sent into the world to be the hands and feet of Jesus.

Chapter 21

WHEN DID I LAST SPEAK TO SOMEONE ABOUT MY FAITH?

Just after the risen Jesus has spent forty days teaching his closest followers about the kingdom of God, he gives them at least two noteworthy challenges. First, Jesus tells his disciples to wait for the Holy Spirit. Jesus has already promised the disciples that the Spirit would lead (and teach, comfort, convict, remind) them as a companion for their journey after Jesus' departure.

Second, Jesus challenges or commissions his disciples to be his witnesses. Jesus tells his disciples that the Holy Spirit will come and empower them, giving them the divine authority to bear witness to the work of Jesus in the world.

When John Wesley challenges us with the question, "When did I last speak to someone about my faith?" he is directly encouraging us to take up the challenge Jesus gave to his disciples in Acts 1:8, to be his witnesses or storytellers. When we share our faith in both word and deed, we fulfill the challenge that Jesus gave the disciples and the church.

Acts 1:8 is not the only place in the Scriptures where we see Jesus commissioning his followers to share their faith, and as a result make disciples. In Matthew 28:18-20, Mark 16:15-16, Luke 24:46-49, and John 20:21-22, Jesus challenges his followers to continue the mission and message of God's work for which he has equipped them. There are three primary elements or common threads found in each of these passages. The common threads are to (1) go, (2) obey, and (3) discern from the Holy Spirit.

To "go" is to look for ways to both proclaim and perform the good news of the gospel—that in Jesus Christ there is redemption. To "go," therefore, is to live on mission, to live as a sent one. The metanarrative (overarching pattern or structure) in the Bible helps us to see the storyline that God the Father sends the Son into the world. God the Father and the Son send the Holy Spirit. God the Father, God the Son, and God the Holy Spirit send the church into the world to bear witness to the work of God. To "go" is to have a way of life in which the good news of the gospel permeates all of your life so that through your daily living as a neighbor, coworker, parent, sibling, or friend, you represent God's love to all those you come into contact with.

To "obey" is to live as Jesus models for us to live. Jesus came not only to die for us but also to show us how to live. Through Jesus' life, death, burial, and resurrection, we see what it means to live a fully human life. Each of us was created with purpose and meaning: to represent God. A fully human life lives into the image of God. To "obey," therefore, is to live toward the purpose and meaning for which we've been created, to live holy lives characterized by love. Simply said, Christians are to journey toward a total love for God and others. When we live for God and others, we obey as Jesus challenged us to do.

To "discern from the Holy Spirit" is, in our obedience to God, to take our direction from God's will. God's will is that the world be made whole. This is why we are sent on a mission to participate with God to restore the world toward its intended wholeness. The Holy Spirit gives us strength, courage, and direction to make the best decisions in our lives to align us with God's mission. The Holy Spirit, our companion for the journey that is life, comforts, teaches, reminds, and convicts us to live a life of obedience. Turning our lives over to God is a constant battle. Jesus wants us to turn our lives over to God so that we might live into God's will rather than our own personal desires.

To respond faithfully to Wesley's question, "When did I last speak about my faith?" is to live a life of going, obeying, and listening to the Holy Spirit, realizing that each one of us is sent into the world to be the hands and feet of Jesus.

It is important to remember that there are two sides of the faith-sharing coin. One side is to proclaim the gospel, to announce it with our words. Jesus clearly shows in the Gospels that we are to be winsome, generous, and open-minded in our proclamation of the gospel. Some of us struggle to proclaim that in Jesus Christ there is salvation because we feel ill-equipped. We fear we don't know enough about the Bible to answer any challenging questions, should they arise. Of course we should consistently be learning and growing in our knowledge of the faith. However, the best story you have to share about the gospel is your own life story of personal transformation. Don't underestimate your personal story of redemption.

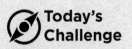

Today's Challenge

Share your faith through your words and actions—or both—today. Actively look for ways to do this. Find the natural opening in a conversation to mention your faith, when before you might have kept your mouth shut. Demonstrate the gospel to someone by blessing them with your actions.

The second side of the faith-sharing coin is performing the gospel. Sharing our faith through acts of mercy, compassion, and social justice is also a key to bearing witness to God's work in the world. When we take time to serve those who are in need, whether with food, shelter, love, safety, or the like, and do it in the name of the Father, Son, and Holy Spirit, we participate with God in God's mission to restore the world toward its intended wholeness.

There are two key aspects of performing the gospel. One is to serve through acts of mercy and compassion. The other aspect is to attack and destroy the systems of injustice in the world. God designs the church (that's you and me, not the building we go to) to be the agency in the world working toward wholeness, and therefore, dismantling darkness. When we participate in justice movements, whether for racial reconciliation, poverty, education, health care, or other causes, we perform the gospel and remind people that God has not forgotten them.

Reflection Questions

1. When *did* you last speak to someone about your faith?
2. Do you show your faith more through your words or deeds? How can you balance both sides of the gospel "coin"?
3. Who first shared his or her faith with you?

Personal Application Ideas

1. Think through your story of personal transformation. How has your faith in God changed your life and made you a better person? Write your story down.
2. If you're not very comfortable speaking about your faith, start small. You don't have to give your testimony to everyone you encounter; that is often a turnoff anyway. Just look for natural openings in conversations, and be willing to answer questions when they arise. People aren't looking for perfect answers. They are looking for *your* answers.

---
scripture

Therefore, go and make disciples of all nations, baptizing them in the name of the Father and of the Son and of the Holy Spirit, teaching them to obey everything that I've commanded you. Look, I myself will be with you every day until the end of this present age.

Matthew 28:19-20

Prayer

God, you sent Jesus to show us the way. Jesus was the way, the truth, and the life. I pray, God, that I would profess my faith and belief in the saving grace of the gospel with courage and direction from the Holy Spirit in order that my family and friends might know that you have not forgotten them with your love. Amen.

NOTES

Chapter 8

1. Carl Sagan, speech at Cornell University, October 13, 1994. See also Carl Sagan, *Pale Blue Dot: A Vision of the Human Future in Space* (New York: Ballantine, 1994), 6.

2. Martin Buber, *Tales of the Hasidim: Later Masters* (New York: Schocken, 1948), 249–50.

Chapter 13

1. http://www.bls.gov/tus/charts/.

Chapter 16

1. http://mashable.com/2012/04/13/elon-musk-secrets-of-effectiveness/#5t.YlTbKMaqE.

Chapter 18

1. A.W. Tozer, *The Crucified Life: How to Live Out a Deeper Christian Experience* (Bloomington, MN: Bethany House, 2011), 200.

ACKNOWLEDGMENTS

I've written a dozen books and worked on many projects like *The Wesley Challenge*. Every time I complete a book or project like this one, I look back and realize how many people have played a huge part in making it happen. This project is no different. I've had a team of incredibly passionate, smart, and gifted people alongside me making what was once merely an idea come to a reality.

I'd like to thank the team of people I work with every day— Michelle and Jeff Kirby, Jane Fowler, Liz Gyori, Darrell Holtz, Michelle Funk, Abby O'Neill, Megan O'Neill, Jill Harqtuist, Debbie Hoskovec, Shari Wilkins, and Chris Abel for all of their input and feedback. I am inspired by your commitment to help people become deeply committed Christians. I am grateful to call each of you my friend.

I'd especially like to thank Bryan Rich, Liz Gyori, Darrell Holtz, and Chris Abel for their creative input and editorial contributions.